HE ASCENDED
INTO HEAVEN

HE ASCENDED INTO HEAVEN

LEARN TO LIVE AN ASCENSION-SHAPED LIFE

Tim Perry

Aaron Perry

PARACLETE PRESS
BREWSTER, MASSACHUSETTS

He Ascended into Heaven: Learn to Live an Ascension-Shaped Life

2010   First Printing

Copyright © 2010 by Aaron Perry and Tim Perry

ISBN: 978-1-55725-631-7

Unless otherwise noted, scriptural references are taken from the *New Revised Standard Version of the Bible*, copyright 1989, 1995 by the Division of Christian Education of the National Council of Churches of Christ in the United States of America and are used by permission. All rights reserved.

Scripture quotations noted with KJV are taken from the King James Version of the Bible.

Scripture quotations noted with NASB are taken from the NEW AMERICAN STANDARD BIBLE®, Copyright © 1960, 1962, 1963, 1968, 1971, 1972, 1973, 1975, 1977, 1995 by The Lockman Foundation. Used by permission.

Scripture quotations noted with ESV are from The Holy Bible, English Standard Version. Copyright © 2001 by Crossway Bibles, a division of Good News Publishers. Used by permission. All rights reserved.

Library of Congress Cataloging-in-Publication Data

Perry, Tim S., 1969-
  He ascended into Heaven : learn to live an ascension-shaped life / Tim Perry, Aaron Perry.
     p. cm.
  Includes bibliographical references.
  ISBN 978-1-55725-631-7
  1. Jesus Christ—Ascension. I. Perry, Aaron Jenkins. II. Title.
  BT500.P47 2010
  232.9'7—dc22   2010013810

10 9 8 7 6 5 4 3 2 1

Published by Paraclete Press
Brewster, Massachusetts
www.paracletepress.com

Printed in the United States of America

For Greg and Rachel, David, and Ruth
They believed when we could not.

For Ken Gavel, Doc Taylor, Melvin McMillen,
Clinton Branscombe, and John Symonds
For keeping theology, biblical studies, and preaching united.

Contents

The Ascension
and the Christian Life

HE ASCENDED
INTO HEAVEN

Preface

Reflecting on the Ascension is necessary, because it suffers from lack of attention in modern times. If the ascension of Jesus is as important as we think it is, why do so many contemporary Christians think so little about it?

A lot of otherwise completely orthodox and very devout people don't bother with the Ascension because, frankly, it's hard to swallow. We allow the questions—themselves provoked by Luke's way of telling the story—in effect, to silence the story. After all, are we really to believe that a literal flesh-and-blood Jesus defied gravity and really rose into the air until a cloud hid him? We've seen far too many portrayals of Jesus floating in wisps of cloudy air to take that image seriously. What happened to Jesus' body after it disappeared? Did it fall back to earth having served its purpose while Jesus' soul left this world behind?

The temptation to drop the ascension story because it appears to ask so much of our ability to suspend disbelief is profoundly real. "He ascended into heaven," after all, is enshrined in the great Creeds, precisely because it is part of the New Testament witness and a central element of historic faith.

To demythologize the Ascension we would have to resort to saying something like this: the Ascension is not only an event in the life of Jesus, but also it is Luke's way of narrating the significance of Jesus' life for his first disciples. It has to do with what Jesus meant to the disciples and, by extension, what Jesus means for us. It is not only a report of what actually happened, it is a statement of the difference Jesus makes in disciples' lives. And since we modern disciples no longer share Luke's belief in a universe of a heaven above and a hell below, the notion of Jesus literally being taken up in glory can be set aside for other, more suitable metaphors. The Ascension is a metaphor that describes the way Christians experience the reign of Jesus in their hearts. It helps us make sense of the fact that Jesus is physically absent and spiritually present to us at the same time.

Of course, this strategy does grasp a deep truth central to this little book: the ascension of Jesus *has* profound implications for the way disciples, whether from the first century, or the twenty-first, live. However, the effort to hang on to the implications while dispensing with the event itself is ultimately in vain. The only way to maintain that the Ascension continues to speak to contemporary followers of Jesus is to begin from the conviction that the Ascension is, in the first instance, something that really happened to Jesus. In his body.

At least, that's what this book hopes to show.

The Ascension
and Jesus

LOOKING UP

CONSIDERING THE ASCENSION OF JESUS

While he [Jesus] was going and they were gazing up toward heaven, suddenly two men in white robes stood by them. They said, "Men of Galilee, why do you stand looking up toward heaven?"
　　—The Acts of the Apostles (1:10–11a)

The Ascension is the festival which confirms the grace of all the other festivals put together—without which the profitableness of every other festival would have perished. For unless the Savior had ascended into heaven, His nativity would have come to nothing . . . and His passion would have born no fruit for us . . . and His most holy resurrection would have been useless.
　　—Saint Augustine

I magine yourself standing alongside the baffled disciples squinting into the sky trying to make sense of what they have just experienced: the ascension of Jesus into heaven. Christians have often found it difficult to stand in

the disciples' place. And yet, the Ascension is included in
the Creeds confessed Sunday after Sunday in churches around
the world. Ascension Day is a feast on many Christian calendars.
Yet few of us have asked: how does this part of the Christian
narrative shape us?

Because the Ascension has not shaped our practice or
vocabulary, we may need to take a longer route to discover
its practical meaning for us. We must really think about
the Ascension. If doubts surface, let them. If the incredible
nature of the story begins to press on our minds and hearts,
we are well on our way. In the midst of the doubts, we must
allow ourselves to wonder just what difference it makes for
our understanding of Jesus. Thinking about ascension is
necessary but insufficient. We only know and understand
the Ascension when we are owned by the ascended Jesus.

New and exciting Christian practices await those who are
shaped by the ascension narrative and its theology. This
shaping, however, does not happen accidentally. It will take
courage and strength of imagination to be taken into this
story—that brings us back to the hillside, the disciples, and
the words of an angel.

"Men of Galilee, why do you stand looking up toward
heaven?" The angel's question comes from the opening scene
of the Acts of the Apostles, the sequel to the Gospel of Luke.
What would it have been like to stand there on the hillside with
the little band that included Peter, Thomas, and the rest, strain-
ing into the sun, hoping to catch one last glimpse of Jesus?

What was going through their minds? Would they have
been asking *our* questions? Were they wondering just where
Jesus went? Were they wondering what would happen next?

Did they have other questions altogether? After all, it had been an amazing few weeks. Jesus had been crucified; he had been raised from the dead, he then spent forty days with them—appearing and disappearing—and now, after some final instructions to them, Jesus rose into the air and was hidden by a cloud.

Let's face it. It's an odd story. Thoughtful, honest, and devout Christians have wondered: Where did Jesus go? Did he enter a realm of premodern spacetravel? Is he living "outside" our universe? Is this story a mythological description of the disciples' awareness that while Jesus was physically dead, he was spiritually alive—at least to them?

If you are asking these or similar questions, you're not necessarily being sceptical or disbelieving. Maybe you are beginning to grapple with a story that Luke knows tests the intellect and accordingly the devotion of authentic Christians. This is a hard story. And it invites hard questions from the start.

Things are further complicated by Luke's way of presenting the event. On the one hand, this event is the climax of his Gospel—it is the event toward which his entire Gospel has been moving. The Ascension is the sign of Jesus' victory—his exaltation. The event is so important to Luke's story that he actually narrates it twice—to end his Gospel and to begin the book of Acts.

Luke wants to leave his readers in no doubt about one simple fact: Jesus left his disciples not through death on the cross, but through conquering death on the cross. The proof of his victory was not only his Resurrection but also his Ascension. It's not that the Resurrection is less important

than the Ascension. It is that, in some way, they are one
continuous divine act. Resurrection is the beginning of
ascension; ascension is resurrection completed.

If Jesus had only been raised from death, then he would
have been like Lazarus—a miracle had been performed—a
man had been raised from the dead, only to come back to
the form of his previous human life. Jesus might have gone
back to Galilee to teach and heal, or he might have—as some
of the disciples hoped on Ascension Day—raised an army to
overthrow the Romans. The miracle would have been no more
than a curious divine detour in the universal human journey
from birth to death.

But in his telling of the Ascension, Luke's point is not so
much that Jesus has been raised from death, but that Jesus has
been raised to a whole new kind of *life* where the old order of
things, dominated by death, is behind him. There would be
no need for more teaching or healing, for the kingdom had
come. There would be no need for armies, because Jesus'
enemies had already been defeated at the cross.

Do you remember reading or perhaps seeing *The Lion, the
Witch, and the Wardrobe* for the first time? How did you feel
when you heard the Stone Table crack? When you stood
with Lucy and Susan staring at the very-much-alive-again
Aslan? When you heard him speak of the "deeper magic from
before the dawn of time" that made death work backwards?
That eruption of crackling joy and deep yearning is what Luke
wants his readers to feel!

This joy is grounded not simply in the story's beauty,
but in its beautiful *truth*. And as truth, our expression of the
Christian faith must be shaped in light of the Ascension

and not simply as a response to our feelings. Luke's Gospel ends with Jesus returning to his Father—enthroned as King of Creation—and the Acts of the Apostles opens with a retelling of the Ascension to remind us that if the old order is defeated, then the disciples, including you and me, are the vanguard of the new order. Luke then calls us, through the rest of the Acts of the Apostles, to be "Ascension people." He invites us to take up the dramatic roles we've been given through the Ascension.

But if this is Luke's point, if the Ascension is clearly a pivotal moment that shapes those who pay attention to it, why does Luke rush past it so quickly? Is Luke afraid his readers—now you and me—will get stuck there on the mountain, stumbling around looking up with our mouths agape, wondering where this kingly Jesus went?

In a word, *Yes*. We could get stuck in such a beautiful place. Luke rushes the story because he doesn't want us to be too comfortable, gazing after the ascended Lord with the first followers of Christ. He wants us talking, writing, thinking, serving, reflecting *because* of the Ascension. So, Luke informs us that two angels appeared and told the disciples to (we paraphrase) "Stop Looking Up!" They told the disciples that Jesus had been taken into heaven and would return in the same way he had left.

What would the disciples have heard in these words? Simply put, they would have been reminded of the risen Jesus' words to them concerning the kingdom during his final forty days with them. Of these teachings, three have been passed to us. Jesus taught his disciples that

♦   the kingdom would indeed arrive, but on the Father's
    timetable, not theirs;

♦   their role in the Father's work required baptism with the
    Holy Spirit; and

♦   the kingdom would expand as the disciples proclaimed
    the Good News in Jerusalem, to the surrounding
    countryside in Judea and Samaria, and eventually to all
    corners of the world.

Notice the unifying theme for these words—imminent
activity. The kingdom *will* come. The Spirit *will* baptize. The
gospel *will* be proclaimed. Now the angel asks, "What on
earth are you waiting for?" There's no time to be looking up;
there's work to do!

Following the angel's own admonition, Luke doesn't want
us stuck on the mountain, either. He wants us to know that
there's still work to do and Luke in the Acts of the Apostles
starts our glimpse at this work. The Spirit empowers ordinary
folks to be gospel witnesses, boldly shouldering their commission, and spreading the Good News from Jerusalem to
Rome, from Jews to Gentiles. Luke wants us talking, writing,
thinking, serving, reflecting *because* of the Ascension; he wants
our current manner of faith reexamined *because* of the Ascension.

Luke wants us to know that evangelism, justice, and mercy
must be spoken and lived in Jesus' name for the poor, violent,
and abused. But such work is only Christian, is only in the
Spirit of Jesus, if it is done in Jesus' name; if it is done in the
name of an ascended first-century Jew. If we neglect, ignore,
or simply forget the Ascension, then the angel will change his
message from "Stop looking up!" to "Stop! Now! Look Up!"

But why? Because the Ascension is a key part of our story. Unlike the disciples, we have lost the ability to believe in and be changed by the Ascension and without it, we neither tell nor live the story rightly. We might be doing good things, but we are not passing on the Good News that's been passed to us.

So, let's ask a question of ourselves—especially if we've been in the church for a long time: how much of our Christian life—how we pray, how we worship corporately, how we witness—draws strength *intentionally* from the Ascension? Could it be the case that even after decades of church life, the answer is none?

Maybe that's not fair. Undoubtedly prayer, worship, politics, and public witness in the life of many churches are shaped in some fashion by Jesus' ascension because their members were passionately concerned about all those things. No doubt many of us can look back on years spent in faithful churches, whether urban or rural, small or large, and be overwhelmed by the strength of faith and practice of these fellowships. We remember Easter testimonies that called us to the joy and hope of resurrection in the face of death; we remember Good Friday sermons that called us to the cross in the face of hostility. But can we remember hearing that the Ascension called us to anything?

The Ascension calls us to look up at Jesus *and* to stop looking up because it is the great transition from the mission of Jesus to the mission of the church. It points up to Jesus and ahead to his disciples—even us! The rest of this book is *both* about looking up *and* looking ahead. As we look up at Jesus, we reconsider key questions: How do we think of Jesus' life and work? How do we think of his death? How do we think of his current absence and presence? But the Ascension forces us to move through Jesus to the mission of the church: How do we think *of ourselves*? How do we call to the world—including how we call to conquered enemies of Jesus who still appear to be in control? How does this seemingly absent Jesus strengthen us in this changed but fallen world?

By asking these questions together, we hope a withered part of our theological imagination will be reinvigorated. But more than this, we hope local churches, local communities of believers, will be reinvigorated, because the church, global and local, should be excited, filled with anticipation of *the present* because of the Ascension.

Look again at Augustine's words about the Ascension that opened our chapter: "[It] is the festival which confirms the grace of all the other festivals put together,—without which the profitableness of every other festival would have perished. For unless the Saviour had ascended into heaven, His nativity would have come to nothing . . . and His passion would have born no fruit for us . . . and His most holy resurrection would have been useless." It seems that the Ascension was quite a big deal in the fifth century! More than Good Friday, Easter, more even than Christmas, Augustine believed that Ascension Day ought to be the climax of our Christian Year.

So, what would it mean for churches to celebrate Jesus' reign? Could we have ascension presents and ascension carols? (Would we stress over shopping days leading up to ascension?) Could public celebrations and games and music and laughter initiate racial reconciliation, enrich the poor and homeless, and uplift the depressed all to celebrate the kingship of Jesus?

These somewhat facetious possibilities abound for new forms of ascension-shaped Christian practice and mission. But first, stop. Let's look up. And then we will follow Jesus into all our Galilees with all the joy the Ascension affords.

DISCUSSION QUESTIONS

1. Augustine said that without the Ascension the Resurrection would have meant nothing. If the Ascension is so important in the Christian narrative, why has it been neglected?
2. The authors say that without being shaped by the Ascension, our lives do not accurately reflect the Good News. Is the Ascension as necessary to the Christian narrative as the authors suggest?
3. Do you agree with the authors' belief that the Ascension changes Jesus' mission so that he no longer needs to teach or heal? Why or why not?
4. What public celebrations could faithfully embody Ascension Day in your community?

2

LOOKING BACK

THE ASCENSION AND THE LIFE OF JESUS

When he ascended up on high, he led captivity captive,
and gave gifts unto men. (Now that he ascended, what
is it but that he also descended first into the lower parts
of the earth? He that descended is the same also that
ascended up far above all heavens, that he might fill all
things.)
    —The Letter to the Ephesians (4:8–10 KJV)

"[This] is how the clues God leaves sometimes work
. . . . Sometimes, as in a great novel, you cannot see until
you get to the end that God was leaving clues for you
all along. Sometimes you wonder, *How did I miss it? Surely
any idiot should have been able to see from the second chapter that
it was Miss Scarlet in the conservatory with the rope.*"
    —Lauren F. Winner

E verybody has a Jesus. Bookshelves in any bookstore
contain popular and academic works on the "Jesus of
history" or "the real Jesus." And every one is different.
Jesus has been a Marxist, an anti-Marxist, a feminist, an

anti-feminist, married, single, and as real as Napoleon and as legendary as Osiris, the Egyptian Judge of the Dead. Jesus, it seems, emerges from the concerns and ideals of the writer. This is nothing new. The nineteenth-century "Jesus of history" looked a lot like a German liberal Protestant: downplaying miracles, stressing morality. As a result, Albert Schweitzer hung a huge question mark over the whole historical Jesus process by saying that all these views of Jesus looked too much like his contemporary scholars and not like the Jesus described in the Gospels. Schweitzer pulled back the curtain of objectivity to reveal the cultural bias behind it. Others have quipped that these views of Jesus are simply the reflections of scholars' faces seen at the bottom of a deep well. They reveal more than bias; they reveal ideology.

While unfortunate, this type of reflection is understandable because Jesus remains a figure of fascination even for those who are not people of Christian, or any, faith. Jesus captivates us. Jesus is beyond our control, and any attempt to describe him with words reveals just how little control he allows us to have. These unintentional self-portraits in Jesus studies tell us that Jesus, more than being the answer, is the question.

What happens if we take a literary approach, reading the Gospels less like a newspaper and more like a historical novel? Would this allow those chronologically nearest to Jesus to provide our best opportunity to understand Jesus' own interpretation of his life and events? If we set aside the questions of history, the what-actually-happened of our curiosity (questions that are important and curiosity that is legitimate) for a moment, could our understanding of Jesus change for the better?

Since Luke's Gospel ends with ascension, we must then ask: how does the end of the story shape what we see going on at its beginning? In its middle? Beyond this, how does employing the Ascension as a hermeneutical practice shape us?

This ascension practice of study is a bit like the film adaptation of Michael Ondaatje's *The English Patient*. One word came to mind: dull. The movie seems to lack story, sequence, and connection from scene to scene and between the characters. Then, in the last ten minutes, everything falls into place. The scenes now fit; the characters' acts and words did, in fact, tell a riveting story. Each scene contained clues that now, in hindsight, engaged the viewers in that last culminating, illuminating moment.

Luke wants the Ascension to evoke a similar experience for his readers. Once we pause with the disciples on the hillside—once we look up—the Ascension acts like a literary flare, casting new light on previous parts of Jesus' story that we may have passed over too quickly. Themes that we otherwise might have missed, in the light of the ascended Christ, become suddenly obvious. Three significant scenes in the story give us a sense of the whole. (A fourth scene—the cross—will be the subject of a whole other chapter.) For now, let's practice ascension-interpretation with three scenes—two from the life of Jesus and one from the life of his Mother—and see how these incidents will shape our understanding.

The Blessed Virgin Mary's words, "Here am I, the servant of the Lord; let it be with me according to your word," capture her heart attitude (Luke 1:38). Some see in these words the posture of passivity that they fear has come to express the general response of women to men. There's ample evidence in Christian history to make such a case. But

how does the end of the story challenge this interpretation?
How does the Ascension demand we reread them? Here are
further words from Mary:

> Surely, from now on all generations will call me blessed;
> for the Mighty One has done great things for me, and
> holy is his name. His mercy is for those who fear him from
> generation to generation. He has shown strength with his
> arm; he has scattered the proud in the thoughts of their
> hearts. He has brought down the powerful from their
> thrones, and lifted up the lowly; he has filled the hungry
> with good things, and sent the rich away empty.
> (Luke 1:48–53)

Did the same woman who confessed herself a servant of
God really speak *these* words? (Hardly the acquiescent Jewish housewife!) Here Mary is acutely aware of being caught
up in the mighty acts of God to rescue his people. But the
two speeches are so different! Indeed, some scholars have
argued that the Magnificat is developed from a hymn that
an early Christian community wrote, obviously *after* the
Ascension, only to be worked by Luke into his narrative.
Whether or not the theory is true is not relevant to this
discussion. In any event we see just how much Mary's Song
is infused with the theme of *divine victory*—with the theme
of the *Ascension*.

Catch the irony of the song in Luke's setting. God is going to display his power, scatter the proud, put down the
mighty, and send the rich away empty-handed. God is going
to exalt the lowly, fill the hungry, and intervene on behalf of

a particular people. God is going to conquer his enemies and right all that is wrong with creation!

How? Through the miraculous conception of his Son in the womb of a Jewish teenager. The birth of a baby is *the* decisive and ultimately victorious act of God.

This irony brings us back to Mary's response to Gabriel. "Here am I, the servant of the Lord." The Greek word we translate servant, *doulos*, doesn't mean a servant, but a slave. But doesn't this emphasize subservience and passivity all the more? Simply put, Mary didn't choose to serve God; God chose her. *Slave* may make us feel uncomfortable, but that's what Mary says.

Now alerted to Luke's ironic reversals, we know that we shouldn't take this title at face value. Who else are God's slaves? In Luke's own writings, Paul and his companions are given that label. In his letters to the church in Corinth, Paul applies this term to all disciples regardless of sex or status. But even more interesting is the use of the term in the Old Testament. Who are the female slaves of the Lord there? Among others there are Deborah, a judge and military leader; Jael, an assassin; and Esther, a queen. Hardly shrinking violets!

When Mary takes the title slave of the Lord, she places herself at the *head* of a long line of *female liberators* of God's people! The Ascension opens our eyes to the theme of conflict and victory right at the beginning. The *victory* of God *is* the One carried by the Blessed Virgin.

The Ascension recasts our interpretation of the life and words of Mary. If Luke expects us to do that with his narrative, shouldn't we do it with our own? We live in an ascension-graced world and our lives must now be interpreted in this light. This means we must treat our own lives like *historical novels* and less like newspapers. Small, perhaps insignificant events in our own lives must now be reexamined.

What details in life do we gloss over? What periods do we skip over quickly when considering our pasts? The Ascension leaves no event darkened; they all warrant reexamination as they are now enlightened by the ascension of Christ. Have you ever experienced moments of insight months or perhaps years after a difficult event? Have you ever seen significant emotional, spiritual, or professional growth only after reflecting on past seasons of trial? Perhaps we can learn to see moments of grace where God had shaped our futures, where previously we only saw pain, inconvenience, perhaps tragedy. Of course God was up to something! How could we have missed it!

Our second opportunity to practice ascension interpretation opens with Jesus rising from Jordan's baptismal waters to hear a heavenly voice declare him to be the "Beloved Son." "Jesus," continues Luke, "full of the Holy Spirit, returned from the Jordan and was led by the Spirit in the wilderness, where for forty days he was tempted by the devil. He ate nothing at all during those days, and when they were over, he was famished" (4:1–2).

Lauren Winner, in *Mudhouse Sabbath*, talks about how fasting weakens and strengthens us simultaneously. The connection between the two is *desire*. We long for food as our bodies are *weakened;* we long for God as our spirits are *strengthened*. Our hunger for food reminds us that our true hunger is for communion with our Creator and Redeemer.

Likewise, we see both physical weakness and spiritual strength in the temptation of Jesus. After having been baptized by John in the Jordan, Jesus left civilization behind to fast for forty days.

Consider the significance of the wilderness. Jesus didn't retreat from people to seek a quiet place to commune with his Father. On the contrary, in Jewish and early Christian thought, the wilderness was the devil's home turf. After fasting for a long time, Jesus was hungry *and* ready to face the tempter's full force. Early Christian readers rightly grasped that the confrontation was a microcosm of Jesus' mission. Here, in the wilderness, before he could begin his work, a decisive battle determined the course, shape, and eventual success of Jesus' mission.

Jesus didn't wind up there by accident. The Gospel writers agree—Jesus went to the wilderness, obeying the call of the Spirit. The conflict Jesus faced did not signal God's abandonment or rejection. He did not go alone. The confrontation with the very personification of evil marked the beginning of Jesus' mission to the world. After God commissioned Jesus at his baptism, Jesus headed off to war.

Scattering the proud and pulling down the mighty has begun!

But of course, and here is Luke's penchant for irony again, *the war would not be fought in the way we usually think.* It is not a contest of equal and opposed powers. Jesus fights by God's rules. Look at Luke's ordering of the three temptations (4:1–10): the devil preys first upon Jesus' hunger and exhaustion. "If you are the Son of God command this stone to become a loaf of bread." The devil tries to break the link between physical and spiritual desire. He hopes to distract Jesus from the sources of spiritual strength by focusing attention on his physical weakness. Jesus' refusal to be baited in this way, though, only increases the intensity of the battle as the tempter moves on to his next tactics.

Next, the devil shows Jesus all the kingdoms of the world and opens to him the route of political power: "To you I will give their glory and all this authority; for it has been given over to me, and I give it to anyone I please."

Finally, the tempter offers the path of religious adoration, when after taking Jesus from the mountain to the temple pinnacle, he says, "If you are the Son of God, throw yourself down from here. . . ."

Perhaps what surprises us most is that Jesus never disagrees with the devil. He doesn't dispute Satan's authority to make these offers or his power to bring them about. Quite the contrary, Jesus takes them as legitimate, yet denies the devil his prize.

These are alluringly and frighteningly real temptations. They are brutal battles. When we stick with the story till the end, this different picture emerges. Luke wants us to know that Jesus faced real temptation from beginning to end and succeeded. Only Jesus felt the tempter's full power to prey upon the weaknesses of the body, will, and spirit. And in each case, Jesus resists only with the words of Holy Scripture and eventually, he is victorious.

Irenaeus, a second-century church father, sees here the beginning of the undoing of the Fall. He plumbs the depths of Paul's title for Jesus, *the second Adam*, by setting the temptation of Adam alongside the temptation of Jesus. Here's how he presents it: Adam and Eve faced the tempter in God's garden. Satan came to their place of advantage. He appealed to their bodies (the fruit was good for food), their wills (the wisdom it held was to be desired), and their spirits (in eating, they would become like God). Where they should have won, they lost, consigning themselves and all their children to live under the reign of God's enemy.

On the contrary, Jesus, the second Adam, faced the tempter in the wilderness. Jesus took the battle to the devil's arena. Far from a mere fruit, Jesus faced a full frontal satanic assault. Satan appealed to his body (make these stones bread), his will (rule over these kingdoms), and his spirit (perform a miracle). With every advantage gone, Jesus should have lost. Yet he defeated Adam's (and our) old enemy. The battle was joined.

Conflict, victory, reversal, irony: where they may have been subtle in Mary's story, now the themes are boldly painted on Luke's canvas. The mission of Jesus is a conflict, a war. And it is not Jesus who is on the defensive. Rather, as he moves from the wilderness into Galilee he's on the *offensive*.

Beginning with this first skirmish in the wilderness, Jesus would proclaim and enact the kingdom of God, rescuing people from the powers of darkness. Every healing, every exorcism, every aphorism and sermon from Galilee to Gethsemane to Golgotha is to be understood as the slow and steady march of the kingdom of God against the devil. And in the end, the Ascension tells us Jesus is *victor*.

We are beginning to see that the image of the battlefield forms Luke's major motif of Jesus' ministry, even his life. Reading Luke's Gospel from the Ascension's perspective sharpens and clarifies this motif. However, there has not yet been a clue in Luke's text that we *should* be reading his Gospel that way. Does Luke want his readers to reread the beginning and middle from the perspective of the end? This question surfaces as we climb another mountain: the Mount of Transfiguration.

This story is almost as strange as the Ascension itself. Luke's account of the Transfiguration begins with Jesus' call to radical discipleship, the call to take up the cross and follow him. Discipleship means losing our lives. Then, these words: "But truly I tell you, there are some standing here who will not taste death before they see the kingdom of God" (Luke 9:27). What does that mean?

Eight days after this discussion, Jesus took Peter, James, and John up a mountain to pray. Uninsightful as they are throughout the Gospel, even these leaders amongst the disciples don't catch the significance of the event. They go to sleep. But Jesus prays, and as he prays he is transformed by God's visible glory—his appearance changes and his robe glistens. Then Moses and Elijah come to talk with him. When the three disciples finally awake, they see Jesus, Moses, and Elijah glorified. They see the kingdom of God well before they die.

Already, there are glimpses of ascension language—the mountain, the glory, the kingdom. All point forward. But there's more. Moses, Elijah, and the transfigured Lord discussed what many modern English Bibles translate as "his departure" and older Bible versions, as "his decease." But what does Luke say? That they talked about *ten exodon autou*. That they talked about Jesus' *exodus*.

What a powerful little word! With it, Luke ties the events that are about to unfold in Jerusalem—the Crucifixion,

Resurrection, and Ascension—to the mightiest act of God in the Old Testament: the rescue of Israel from Pharaoh's misrule. The God who brought Israel *up* from Egypt is about to bring Jesus *up* from Jerusalem!

Finally, in a wonderful example of foreshadowing, Luke writes that the sleepy-eyed disciples then asked if they could stay there on the mountain. Peter, James, and John, with their babbling about building houses, did not grasp until later, on another mountain, that Jesus was *going up*. And in so doing, he was going to complete the miraculous work God began when Israel was taken up from Egypt to the Land of Promise.

Jesus' victory, the display of his glory, the fullness of the kingdom, *is* Jesus' being taken up to sit at God's right hand. *It is the Ascension*. We cannot avoid this battlefield-shaped image of the Savior. Does this change your image of Jesus?

For many, Jesus conjures up images of a slightly effeminate, unswervingly kind man who knocks on hearts' doors and travels around Galilee smiling at children and carrying lambs. This Jesus has sandy brown hair and blue eyes. He is tall and thin. Mental and theological maturity only develops this image. Jesus becomes wise, full of catchy clichés, sometimes confusing, and not quite with the rest of us. Jesus is not really human. This Jesus is the evangelical image of Gnosticism.

How so? Just as the earliest Gnostics couldn't bring themselves to affirm Jesus' humanity because flesh was bad, this domesticated Jesus tames the Incarnation. Jesus is God. Just as the earliest Gnostics thought that salvation meant escape from this world, escape from being human, this domesticated Jesus is either not human, or at best, only partly human. This domesticated Jesus, being less than fully human, betrays the Jesus who is God's own human story.

Perhaps Gnosticism is a heresy peculiar to those of us who have grown up in ascension-negligent churches. When ascension-interpretation is practiced, however, our image of Jesus can never be so safe.

A domesticated Jesus makes domesticated Christians. Domesticated preachers preach good principles to Christians. Domesticated churches make nicer sinners and confuse the American dream that has seeped into many cultures by attempting to give it God's blessing. A domesticated Jesus makes Christians who can win friends and influence people, but not much more.

What happens when we practice an ascension-interpretation of Jesus? We start to see *our own* lives in battle.

Could the sexual exploitation of both men and women in our culture be the enemy's means of physical temptation in our generation, just as Jesus was tempted to turn stones to bread?

Could the contemporary political engagement of the religious right *and* now the religious left be the enemy's temptation that overly optimistic futures lie within our grasp?

Could the desire to shine and polish performance in contemporary worship be the enemy's temptation for religious success?

These temptations are not easily recognized as such; the goods offered are not bad. Sex is a gift of God. Political structures that provide means of change are gifts of God. Abilities to lead engaging worship regardless of tradition, preach compellingly, and raise funds are gifts of God. Yet when we practice ascension-interpretation, seeing Jesus' temptations as *battles*, we know that our lives are battles, too. Every good and perfect gift comes from God, but the Incarnation reminds us that good and perfect gifts come wrapped in flesh that is tempted to fail. But always flesh that, the Cappadocian Fathers taught us so well, has been fully assumed and is capable of living in the power of the Spirit.

Having learned *irony* via the Ascension from Luke, perhaps we can say it like this: the Ascension *grounds us*—it makes us discerning. The Ascension is also the *ground* of our hope. The victory of *Christ* means that we can boldly ask questions such as:

♦ In what ways should Christians practice celibacy (or other forms of fasting) in a sex-crazed culture, because Jesus—who gave up everything—has been vindicated?

♦ What politics can Christians practice that offer tangible change in or through parliament, council, or the White House because Jesus is already ascended?

♦ What faithful witness can be reclaimed that has previously been sacrificed, perhaps unwittingly, for ecclesial influence and power—something we now see as unnecessary because of the Ascension?

♦ With discernment and hope, we fight boldly—aware that gifts can be misconstrued, cognizant that our lives involve battles, humbled that we will lose at times, inspired that Jesus, in spite of all the disadvantages given to him by Adam, has taken the fight to the devil's home turf and emerged victorious—because Jesus' victory is our victory.

DISCUSSION QUESTIONS

1. Have you ever read the Gospel of Luke as an historical novel? What opportunities does this reading create? What challenges does this reading pose?

2. What challenges do present-day Christians face that should be considered *battles*? How is this true in your life?

3. Can you see what is meant by a "domesticated Jesus"? How has your picture of Jesus changed?

4. Do you see elements of the Exodus in Jesus' transfiguration. Read Luke 9:28–36. What other elements from the Exodus narrative might be present in this event?

5. Is it appropriate to read the life of Mary in light of Jael, Esther, and Deborah? How might this picture shape our visions of female leadership in the church?

3

LOOKING AT

THE ASCENSION AND THE DEATH OF JESUS

When he had made purification for sins, he sat down at the right hand of the Majesty on high, having become as much superior to angels as the name he has inherited is more excellent than theirs.

—The Letter to the Hebrews (1:3b–4)

For the gift, being truly great, was made even greater by the fact that it was through the Son. For in saying "he sat down on the right hand" and having by himself "made purification for our sins," though he had put us in mind of the cross, he quickly added the mention of the resurrection and ascension. And see his unspeakable wisdom. He did not say "he was commanded to sit down" but "he sat down."

—John Chrysostom

A

ll of this talk about the victory of Jesus ought to catch in our throats when we move to the Passion of Jesus—to his cross, though perhaps it's hard, after almost 1,700 years of acceptability to understand why.

When you imagine a cross—whether it's the budded cross of Orthodoxy, the Catholic crucifix, the Celtic knotted rood, or some other representation—what do you see?

In the fourth century, the Roman Emperor Constantine dreamed of a blood-red cross, and heard these words: "In this sign conquer." He went on to win a battle that cemented his claim to the Empire's throne. After the Battle of Milvian Bridge, Constantine moved Christianity to the center of Roman life and the cross became a culturally acceptable symbol. What was once unacceptable soon became ubiquitous and once ubiquitous, meaningless. The last millennium and a half has seen the cross move from a military marker, to a cultural identifier, to a piece of jewelry. It has gone from adorning shields and flags to the necks of professional soccer players and rock stars.

What would happen, asks American theologian William Placher, were Christians to remove the crosses from our church steeples, from behind our altars and communion tables and pulpits, and install instead miniature but otherwise fully functional electric chairs? Perhaps pastors and priests would find their e-mail inboxes flooded with genuine questions of décor, being relevant, and being seeker friendly. We hope though that those questions would provide the dialogue in which those churches could see the cross as their ancestors did in the first three centuries of the Christian faith.

For our ancestors, the cross symbolized the power of the state to take a life—not just take it, but to do so in the most humiliating way possible. It was the Roman Empire's way of sending a message. Hanging naked and exposed sometimes for days, dying of asphyxiation, while the crucified victim's torment is silently screamed to all who witnessed it, "They can, they will, and you might be next."

No wonder it took centuries for crosses to become common in Christian art. We find fish, loaves, sheep, and other images drawn from the Eucharist or the Gospels scattered among early Christian homes, graves, and places of worship—but very few crosses. A cross behind an early Christian altar would make as much sense to them as an electric chair behind our altar would to us.

And Luke seems to confirm that understanding. The opening chapters of his Gospel are a catalog of victories— miracles of healing and exorcism, calling the disciples, more miracles, parables, yet more miracles, the Twelve commissioned and sent out to carry on the work of healing and teaching. Jesus looks very much like the on-the-offensive holy warrior. The kingdom of God is advancing; its enemies exposed and exorcized. And Peter finally gets it. He knows who Jesus is and he has to shout it out. "You are the Messiah of God!"

Then things turn dark. Jesus begins to talk about death; his death. The miracles begin to dwindle—so do the followers. The conflict with the religious leaders begins to grow in intensity. He compares the lawyers, the Pharisees, and the rest of the Jewish leaders to those who killed the prophets. These leaders begin to plot Jesus' murder. The parables become more haunting: finding the narrow door, the rich man in hell.

Then, as the story of Jesus moves to its climax, he is slowly stripped of all he holds dear. In Gethsemane, his disciples abandon him—first in sleepiness and then in fear. He is betrayed. He is tossed from one court to another.

When the verdict is finally passed, it is not by any religious or political authority, but by a mob. And Jesus is crucified. All his companions, writes Luke, including the women who had followed him from Galilee, stood *at a distance, watching*.

Through Luke's telling of the terrible events, Jesus retains his inscrutable nobility. He refuses to be drawn in by taunts from religious leaders, crowds, and soldiers. He passes the opportunity to condemn Peter in mid-denial. He remains silent in the face of false accusation. He prays for his executioners. He forgives the penitent thief. But Jesus' nobility appears ultimately tragic. His is the nobility of the beautiful but lost cause.

Luke's story seems to end as it began: Where Jesus was once swaddled and laid in a stone feeding trough, now he is again swaddled and laid in a rock-hewn tomb. "Here lies Jesus. Martyr." A terse, true epitaph for a Friday afternoon.

But Luke's story of Jesus' earthly life doesn't end there. It ends with the Ascension. And with ascension eyes, we begin to see more to the story than the trope of the tragic hero undone by his own inability to compromise.

Ascension eyes see in the deepening darkness moments of hope, such as the Transfiguration. And now we see another: when the time came for him *to be taken up*, writes Luke, Jesus set his face toward Jerusalem. There is no mistaking the tragedy that will unfold, but the tragic elements are not the whole story. The cross is cast with Jesus' ascension, showing that on the cross, tragedy and triumph come together.

The orchestrated murder of an innocent man is perhaps the greatest possible tragedy. It is tragic that Jesus dies, that he dies alone, that in dying, he bears in his body the rejection of

Jew and Gentile alike. *And it is a triumph.* It is the completion of the Exodus, the mighty act of God to rescue his people from God's enemies. It is his victory over the way the world rules. It is his moment of total faithfulness when all others have scattered. "The cross is foolishness to those who are perishing," Paul wrote to the Christians in Corinth, "but to us who are being saved it is the power of God" (1 Corinthians 1:18). The cross conveyed degradation and death. *But* it is the symbol of Jesus' victory. And as both, it belongs at the heart of our worship.

Sometimes that cuts across our way of thinking about the cross. Sometimes Christians speak of the resurrection and ascension of Jesus as though they undo the Cross, as though the Cross was, in fact, Jesus' (albeit temporary) defeat by the principalities and powers.

Have you ever heard the gospel song "The Champion"? It retells the Gospel as a boxing match. Jesus versus the devil. Angels and demons pack the celestial stands while God the Father referees. It's a close-fought fight until Satan lands a sneaky sucker punch that fells the Lord. And amidst angelic and demonic silence, God starts to count: "10 . . . 9 . . . 8 . . . 7." Satan knows the match is drawing to a close: God is counting *backwards*. Jesus is raised and Satan's victory is forever denied. The resurrection and ascension of Jesus, says the song, undo the Cross.

And that is the opposite of the message of the New Testament. While the New Testament gives us no *single* doctrine of atonement, no one systematic theological way to think about what happened on the cross, all of its metaphors agree that the Cross is no obstacle to God's saving work. When Paul writes to Christians in Corinth that he wanted to know only Christ crucified, that the message of the Cross was the wisdom and power of God, we know the Cross is primary.

Here we see the great upside-down world of God's economy. The Cross re-arranges the world from its deepest foundations up. The Ascension is the announcement that the rearrangement has begun. In the light of the Ascension, the Cross is the capstone of a victorious life.

Cross and ascension, united in Hebrews, form its dominant motifs. "After making purification for sins, he sat down at the right hand of the Majesty on high" (Hebrews 1:3 ESV). The purification of sins is a metaphor for the cleansing power of the sacrifice of Jesus on the cross, and this sacrifice's efficacy is captured in three little words: *He sat down*. They come from Psalm 110:1; "The Lord says to my lord, 'Sit at my right hand until I make your enemies your footstool.'" This begins a militant hymn in which God actively opposes the king's enemies and grants the king victory. Throughout the New Testament, this psalm, this one verse, and even these three little words, function as a shorthand description of the work of Jesus.

The author of Hebrews uses the words to invite readers both to look back at the Cross and ahead to the Ascension. When we look back, we see the Cross and its horror. When we look ahead, we see the seated Christ and know that nothing supplements nor undoes his work. When we look ahead, we are invited to see Jesus enthroned—yet even now reigning over a renewed creation in which all creation sings the praises of God!

But doesn't this sound too easy? Don't we see evidence to the contrary? Don't wars in Iraq and Afghanistan, the seemingly perpetual conflict between Israel and Palestine, civil strife in Zaire and Zimbabwe tell us that the reign of Jesus is just not *that* established? The list of countries where people have been harmed by violence fills pages. The quest for peace—real social harmony rooted in the forgiveness of enemies—in these places seems futile; the best that can be hoped for, the politicians tell us, is a decline in violence secured by the threat of greater violence.

In 2007–2008, this threat of greater violence was given a deceptively simple name: "The Surge." The Surge referred to the thousands of additional American troops dispatched to Iraq to prevent the country from sliding into a civil war. By 2009, it appeared to have worked. Iraq gained an air of stability. Stable enough, in fact, to begin a draw-down of troops. The Surge (and any and all wars, conflict, violence, and oppression) makes us question the Ascension.

And the Surge speaks against the Cross. On the one hand, we, as disciples of Jesus, might be happy that as a result of the Surge, girls in Iraq may (more) safely go to school, vendors may open their shops, and the public may browse the bazaars without fear of being shelled or bombed. On the other hand, it saddens us, especially the followers of the Prince of Peace, that this surge tactic appears the best humanity can do. There may be a reduction in violence, but it is a peace achieved through superior firepower. That is not the same as atonement, reconciliation, resolution, or forgiveness. That is not real peace that the Cross, we believe, has won.

The power and authenticity of this objection is obvious, as the author of Hebrews was also aware. He acknowledges that we do not see the world as the Ascension says it really is, and he guides us to the eighth psalm for direction. This hymn blesses God for the dignity with which God has crowned human beings. Listen to some of its words: "[W]hat are human beings that you are mindful of them, mortals that you care for them? Yet you have made them a little lower than God; and crowned them with glory and honor. . . . [Y]ou have put everything under their feet" (Hebrews 2:6–7). Human beings are to be seen as the crown of God's material creation.

The author of Hebrews, however, straightforwardly acknowledges that we do not see ourselves in this way. It is not immediately obvious that human beings have been made just a little lower than the angels and crowned with glory and honor. "But," the writer continues, "we do see Jesus . . . now crowned with glory and honor because of the suffering of death" (Hebrews 2:9). With the writer, we see Jesus, even now, reigning; when a new believer is baptized; when we break bread and take the cup together; when churches live in a spirit of mutual submission.

All of these gifts are from the ascended Jesus, because they inaugurate and exemplify the community that is meant to reign with Jesus. This means that the best place to look for the truth of the Ascension is in the community that *lives in the truth of the Cross*. Local churches live into the Ascension by living faithfully and unashamedly the life of the Cross. Churches that live in victory gained any other way are putting asunder what Luke and the writer of Hebrews have joined together.

Local churches live into the Ascension by being, by the world's account, a peculiar, even failing, community. By this we do not mean that local churches should be small, pathetic, uneducated, and unprofessional. We mean that these communities should do things that make the world wonder how they continue to exist. Things such as sending shoe boxes filled with gifts around the world to kids they will never meet; such as spending money to feed people who will never contribute to their community financially; such as visiting, possibly accepting as members, inmates who may never get out of prison. This is not to denigrate the operating budgets of local churches, but it is to say that the Ascension reminds us the way of the cross is victorious even without appearing that way.

In 2006, several counties in southern New York State suffered a significant flood. Many homes and businesses were ruined or significantly damaged. Members of Calvary Community Church, where I, Aaron, served as an associate pastor, spent two days cleaning out a flooded motel, owned by Buddhists, and their adjacent home. Workers hauled beds and desks and TVs from marshy, muddy rooms, through the mud-caked parking lot, to the curb. They hauled mud-slimed beer cans that the gracious owners accepted as partial payment for one of the tenant's rent. They emptied mud-flooded washing machines of muddy clothes. After two days and hundreds of man-hours invested in the cleanup, officials condemned the motel and it was razed. By the world's standards, that work was a failure. Or at best pointless. But in light of the Ascension and the Cross, that work has eternal value. Because the Ascension makes the Cross the capstone of a victorious life, events that have no significant, immediate, or tangible payoff are still victories.

As such, the Ascension demands that cruciform living be intentional. The cross was not an ugly aside to the life of Jesus; the Ascension, as we have said, confirms it as the capstone. Unless there is real sacrifice, the Cross is not our way of life and the Ascension has been forgotten. Yet because of the Ascension—a public display of power—Christians do not abandon all forms of power, only the manner in which they are used. The lives and possibly professions of wealthy, educated, influential Christians should make the world wonder why these assets are never used to the Christian's own advantage.

Two accounts illustrate this intentional, ascension-shaped sacrificial life. Rodney Stark has shown how the Christian response to the Plague of Galen provided Christianity's exponential growth. Andy Crouch writes, "In the face of terrible conditions, pagan elites and their priests simply fled the cities. The only functioning social network left behind was the church, which provided basic nursing care to Christians and non-Christians alike, along with a hope that transcended death." Crouch then quotes Dionysius: "Many died in their stead. The best of our brothers lost their lives in this manner, a number of presbyters, deacons, and laymen winning high commendation so that death in this form . . . seems in every way the equal of martyrdom." Many of those to whom Christians showed care died. Some lived and converted. Others saw their family cared for by Christians and converted. That practice of care is exemplary of ascension-shaped cruciform living.

The second account is of the Rev. Ben Kwashi, the Anglican Bishop of Jos, Nigeria, who oversees a diocese in Nigeria's central plateau state, where Christian/Muslim tensions are constantly simmering. Tensions that have claimed thousands of lives since 2001. These tensions have resulted in terrible violence being visited directly upon Ben himself, his wife, and his family. Bishop Ben lives—really lives—in a world in which the victory of Jesus seems to be *impossible*.

At one point, Bishop Ben and his wife were waiting in the Los Angeles airport for their return flight to Jos after his wife had come to America for medical treatment as a result of injuries sustained during a religiously driven assault. As they waited to board their plane, a young African-American man approached him. "He saw my color and my collar and he came to talk to me," Ben said.

"Why," said the young man "is there so much violence? Why do black men kill each other? Why are there so many guns?" Bishop Ben answered, "I do not know. But I do know this. When I go to heaven, I am going to ask Jesus just these questions." He then paused and looked at the man. "Why don't you come to heaven with me and we will ask him together?" In the next moments, Bishop Ben and the young man knelt and prayed that he might be given the gift of faith that he could see Jesus sitting at the Father's right hand.

Bishop Ben and our Christian ancestors exemplify ascension-shaped cruciform living. Unparalleled opportunities for gracious and lavish cruciform love present themselves in our world once we are shaped by the Ascension. The world sees disaster, futility, epidemic, and danger. In light of the Ascension, Christians see victories!

DISCUSSION QUESTIONS

1. We have argued that the Cross is the victory of Christ; that it is *not* undone by the Resurrection and Ascension. Have you considered that the Resurrection and Ascension undo the Cross? How has this chapter challenged this way of thinking?

2. In what ways could your local expression of Jesus' life be practicing cruciform living? In what ways could you begin to live intentionally in a cruciform manner?

3. The authors believe that actions that have no "cash value" can still reflect the cross-life and as such must be considered victorious. Do you agree or disagree? Why or why not?

4. In the teaching of the sheep and the goats (Matthew 25:31–46), Jesus promises to return in glory and bring judgment. Look at the list of kind deeds that he accepts as service to himself. What deeds could you add to this list from your community—deeds that have no apparent pay-off?

4

TAKEN UP

THE ASCENSION AND THE ABSENCE OF JESUS

Then he led them out as far as Bethany, and lifting up his hands, he blessed them. While he was blessing them, he withdrew from them and was carried up into heaven. And they worshiped him, and returned to Jerusalem with great joy; and they were continually in the temple blessing God. Amen.

—The Gospel of Luke (24:50–53)

He was carried up unto heaven, that He might share the Father's throne even with the flesh that was united unto Him. And this new pathway the Word made for us when he appeared in human form. And hereafter in due time He will come again in the glory of His Father with the angels, and will take us up to be with Him.

—Cyril of Alexandria

M y family and I (Tim) used to live in a split-level house in Otterburne, Manitoba, a rural Canadian community near the Manitoba–North Dakota border. It was a lovely property bordered by a forest and a river, the home being built and well-lived-in by only one other family since 1970. Nearing the end of the process of purchasing the house some slightly unsettling history came to light.

The house was first built on a simple concrete pad, with no piers to underpin or stabilize it. With no foundational support and being near a river, the house began to shift so seriously that the physical integrity of the entire structure was threatened. To fix the problem, the previous owners cleverly excavated around the original pad and poured concrete pillars alongside to underpin it. The house was stabilized and continues to stand firm today.

In July of 2007, these concrete pillars took on new meaning. You could have been by the spot hundreds of times, playing with kids, cutting the grass, hosting a barbeque, but have never seen the small message. On the top of one of those pillars was a pint-sized handprint. Underneath it, clearly written with a stick in the fresh cement, was the name "Mark." Mark, the only son of the first owners, was now frozen in time, at this space in concrete form. Though years have passed, on the top of this pillar is, and will continue to be, the handprint of a little boy.

Staring into such a frozen moment, one can lose track of time because that handprint is about memory and presence. The moment created such a personal, powerful, evocative image that when I had a back deck installed later that summer, I had my children put their hands and feet in another set of wet concrete pillars. The concrete now forever bears the presence of Calvin, Sara, and Hugh. Thirty-seven years later, my children joined Mark in an impromptu memorial to their childhoods. As long as their handprints are visible, they will be present in that house. No matter where life takes my children, that house will remember them just as they were that summer.

There's a sense in which Mark's handprint, along with those of my children, provide us with an analogy that helps us get to the heart of the meaning of the Ascension, namely: the paradox that Jesus is ascended and therefore both absent from us and yet present to us.

On the one hand, Jesus is gone. He has ascended bodily into heaven. He has left us. On the other hand, he remains present by the Holy Spirit. He has left reminders of his presence in his Word and in the signs and seals of sacraments— signs as physical—as material as concrete, and as water, bread, and wine.

As we reflect on this paradox, our emotional response might be *Sensucht*. In German, this means something like longing, nostalgia, hope, and memory all mingled together. It combines both a looking forward and a looking back. C.S. Lewis called it *joy*. And this sort of *joy* ought to be the defining characteristic of Christ's followers living in the light of the Ascension.

Though, in another sense the handprint analogy is dangerously misleading. For Mark—wherever he is—is no longer the little boy sinking his hand into wet cement. Two years have passed for Calvin, Sara, and Hugh and, even though it's hardly comparable to the decades in Mark's case, they are now, in many ways, different people.

The people who left those signs are absent. The presence they have left behind is ethereal, elusive, even illusory. In the cold hard world of material reality, they are only memories. They have no existence beyond what we can give them as we contemplate them. They are gone.

So, the analogy breaks down at just this point. When we come down the mountain with the disciples on Ascension Day, it's clear that Jesus is no mere memory, no ghostly presence conjured up by physical reminders of his former days. The disciples returned to Jerusalem in great joy! Contained within that joy was a longing to see Jesus again. But here was more than the wistful nostalgia associated with concrete moments frozen in time. Their joy was a powerful desire impelling them into the future. Because Jesus had ascended into heaven, the disciples were sure not only that they would see him again, but also that he would be present with and to them until their faith was rewarded with sight.

Certainly, that's how Luke's account reads. The Ascension is the great secret toward which he's been building. This revelation is the climax of the Good News that Luke has received from eyewitnesses and servants of the Word: the Lord has triumphed, and as a result, all of creation will be and is being recovered. In the Acts of the Apostles, we see Jesus receive his kingdom, the prize he was awarded when he returned to the Father.

If we imagine ourselves in Luke's story here, as we walk back to Jerusalem with the joyous disciples, we can look back over the whole of Luke's story and see that he has been leading us toward this revolutionary realization all along. The clues are starting to make sense. The completion of the mission of the Son for Luke is not the Cross, and not even the Resurrection. The completion of Christ's mission is the

Ascension, because it is the enthronement of the Son of Man, victorious over his enemies by the Cross, to reign over his endless kingdom.

Jesus has returned to his Father. But if he has returned to his Father in this way, then surely the most obvious implication is that he has, in some sense, left us. And yet, Jesus' absence is not one to mourn. The disciples come back to Jerusalem to worship, expecting the coming of the one whom Luke says is "the promise of the Father." The story of Jesus' ascension, of his absence, is not simply good news, but the very best of news.

Here's why.

Luke begins his account of the Ascension this way: "Then he led them out as far as Bethany, and, lifting up his hands, he blessed them" (24:50). This blessing seems like a relatively small act, yet it is clear that Luke wants us to notice it. He mentions it twice in a very short space, accenting the fact that it was the last act before Jesus' dramatic departure. This simple act of blessing is, in the words of the biblical scholar Joel B. Green, "the finale of his earthly sojourn with his followers."

In the biblical narrative, the bestowal of blessing is a powerful, often concluding moment. Blessing frequently signals the end of one movement of the story and the beginning of another, the end of one character's dealings with God and God's persistence with the next generation of his children. Luke, as a master storyteller, knows this very well. He is confident that his readers will, upon reading about this final blessing, call to mind the last acts of other leaders in the narrative of God's dealing with his people.

There is probably a faint echo of the blessing given by Isaac to Jacob and Esau, whose words, even unintentionally, shaped

the destinies of both sons. Stronger yet is the allusion to
Jacob's last act: blessing his sons and grandsons shortly before
he died. Again, these are no mere final words intended to evoke
nostalgia. Rather, they announced the future shape not only of
the lives of the men on whom Jacob laid his hands, but also
those of their families and even future descendents.

Most explicit, though, is Luke's allusion to the conclusion
of Moses' story in the book of Deuteronomy. Moses' final
words form the conclusion to the one great ascension story
of the Old Testament that Luke has already woven into his
own narrative fabric: the bringing *up* of Israel from Egypt,
from the land of slavery to the land of promise. Yet even more
than that, Moses' dénouement, itself an ascension story, is the
backdrop upon which Luke draws most. The great liberator
and lawgiver brings Israel's descendants to the end of their
wilderness wandering. He and they find themselves on the
threshold of the Promised Land. Moses knows he will not go
into the land with the people. New leaders will soon emerge
to guide them. The story of God's dealings with Israel is about
to enter a whole new chapter.

As a last great act, Moses gathers the people in the plains of
Moab and blesses them, tribe by tribe. Reuben, Judah, Levi,
Benjamin, Joseph . . . one by one, Moses calls the people by
their ancestral names, announcing where they will live
and how they will prosper in the new land. His words are
largely optimistic, ending with a collective description of
Israel's excellence and the glory of Israel's mighty God.

Forty years of leadership draw to a close with this speech.
It is time for Moses to depart. And he does so in a most strik-
ing way, at least for a Christian reader. Moses *went up* from the

plains of Moab to the top of Mount Pisgah (Deuteronomy 34:1). There, God showed Moses the land to which he had led the children of Israel, and when Moses died, God buried him in a secret sepulcher.

With these and other biblical blessings flitting like shadows at the margins of his Gospel, Luke invites us to reflect on Jesus' last words with a greater sense of urgency. For when uttered as a *blessing*, we see more clearly that these are Jesus' *last* words. Just like the last words of Isaac, Jacob, and Moses in many ways foreshadowed or even determined the destiny of their descendants, so Jesus' last words are to be understood as a blessing that foretells and will forever shape the destiny of those who would follow him.

His words of blessing begin with a promise—once Jesus has returned to heaven, he will send the Father's gift—and they continue with a command—having received the Father's gift, the disciples will bear witness to all that they have seen and heard about Jesus. Just what the gift is, Luke does not say explicitly. He does, though, give us a clue, describing the gift as "power from on high" (24:49b).

By now we are not surprised to discover that these four words capture an essential part of the Old Testament story. They call to mind words from the book of the prophet Isaiah that speak of God's land being torn by conflict and made barren by war "until a *spirit from on high* is poured out on us" (Isaiah 32:15). Only after this healing, restorative Spirit is poured out, will peace, righteousness, and social harmony return.

The promise of the Father, the gift for which Luke's disciples are to wait, is revealed to be the Holy Spirit, the Spirit of God, who will come in the end time to set all that is wrong to right, to pacify the warlike, and to render the land fruitful once again. This wonderful universal renewal of creation, Luke tells us, is now possible because of the ascension of Jesus.

Luke wants us to comprehend the coming of the Spirit as the earthly echo of the heavenly enthronement of the victorious Son. Jesus is the heavenly king and as such, he is absent. Through the coming of the Spirit, though, he remains present with his followers. The coming of the Holy Spirit, the promised power from on high, is the sign and guarantee of Jesus' reign and the manner of Jesus' continued presence.

The blessing, rich in biblical imagery and eschatological hope, ends. Like the children of Israel on the doorstep of Abraham's Promised Land, the disciples stand at the outset of their own mission. It is time for Jesus to go. It is time for him, like Moses and Israel, to be *taken up*. Luke describes it like this: Jesus "withdrew from them and was carried up into heaven" (24:51).

Yet, it will not do to spiritualize these four little words—*he withdrew from them*—to use them to say that Jesus laid aside his body so that he could be present with all his followers in a more spiritual, even more intimate way. No. Jesus was withdrawn from his disciples. Jesus, in his humanity, remains withdrawn from us.

People mark significant departures, both real and anticipated. Perhaps the most significant marker for the weightiest parting is the funeral. Across time and culture, human beings find ways to mark the parting that comes with death and to express its accompanying grief. This heaviness overshadows even the most happy of occasions. In the midst of the joy of watching the birth of children, parents may experience terrible awareness not only of their own mortality, but also that of their newborn child. We all know departures well.

Luke tells us that Jesus' departure was different. Jesus was parted from us not by death, but because he was "carried up into heaven." In the appendix, we touch on the cosmological questions this little phrase tempts us to explore. But vital to Luke's Gospel is not the cosmology this phrase may (or may not) express as much as the theological weight it carries. Jesus was carried up not so much because "up there" was where God lived, but because he was elevated, exalted to sit on the throne that, we were told by the angel Gabriel in the Annunciation, was his birthright. *It is a declaration of status far more than it is a determination of location.*

This reign of King Jesus was foreshadowed in the transfiguration story, at that time revealed only to three: Peter, James, and John (Luke 9:27-36). Now it is made plain to all of the disciples. None of those who were present at the Ascension can escape the conclusion that the one whom they had abandoned, whom the mob condemned, whom the elite handed over, whom the Romans had murdered, in fact turned the tables on these principalities and powers.

In his faithfulness to his mission to the end, Jesus defeats the powers of Satan. Because he defeats them, he receives divine approval and reward. No wonder that within two or three decades, early Jewish Christian communities would begin to sing hymns to Jesus that proclaimed his exaltation to reign as the reward for his obedience to his mission, for his refusal to take advantage of the divine power that was his, opting instead for the form of a servant and the mission of the cross.

The disciples could sing such songs of proclamation because the Ascension made it plain that the humility and humiliation of Jesus were not the final word on Jesus' story. The verdict of the powers that put Jesus to death had been decisively overturned by God's own verdict. God determined this life and death to be a victory, one in which the principalities and powers are undone by their own overgrasping.

To proclaim and reward this winning of the war, God did not simply restore his Son to life, but made him the king spoken of by the prophet Daniel: "To him was given dominion and glory and kingship, that all peoples, nations, and languages should serve him. His dominion is an everlasting dominion that shall not pass away, and his kingship is one that shall never be destroyed" (7:14).

Yet all of this victory, all of this celebration, means that Jesus was parted from them. Jesus was carried up into heaven. How did the disciples react? Luke puts it this way: "And they worshiped him, and returned to Jerusalem with great joy; and they were continually in the temple blessing God" (24:52–53). And he adds his own note of agreement: "Amen."

The disciples' initial reaction is to worship Jesus. No wonder. They had finally come to understand just who Jesus is. He was the prophet who proclaimed God's reign and the king who presides over God's kingdom. But they saw him as more than that. In those roles, he was one worthy of worship. They worshiped Jesus.

This response is unprecedented in Luke's Gospel. It is usually the case that when people responded to the saving activity of Jesus, they did so by worshiping God. Now, however, the disciples—Jews who worshiped the one and only God and counted all other deities as false gods—are so overwhelmed by the ascension of Jesus and what it declares about him, that they worship *him*. They thus express their deep conviction that in Jesus they have encountered not simply a prophet or a king, not even the Messiah of Israel, but they have encountered the God of Abraham, Isaac, and Jacob in so direct and profound a way that the only response is to worship.

Worship then gives way to joyful obedience. King Jesus commanded them to stay in Jerusalem until they had received the Spirit (Luke 24:49). And having worshiped the king as he entered into his reign, they were obedient. Luke leaves us anticipating what comes next. The Ascension marks both the completion of the Son's mission and the beginning of the mission of his followers—to bear witness to his triumph. Luke leaves us hoping for a sequel to his story—that, of course, is the Acts of the Apostles.

These followers of Jesus, having seen what they had, having seen the one who was crucified alive again, and not just alive, but exalted to God's throne and beginning to reign in God's kingdom, would not—could not—conceal their obedience in the privacy of their homes or rooms. They would take their worship of the crucified, risen, and ascended one to the center of their community's religious and public life: to the temple.

In public they will worship. In public they will praise. In public they will wait. And we wait with them for the gift of the Holy Spirit, whose coming will inaugurate the mission of the church: the taking of the gospel to Jerusalem, to Judea and Samaria, and to the uttermost parts of the earth. Jesus' victory is the property of no one culture or ethnicity.

As the victory of the second Adam, it is the victory of all of Adam's children. It is your victory and mine.

In the light of the first celebration of Jesus' victory, Luke's own "Amen" might leave us feeling a little anticlimactic. Why not just fade to black with the disciples in the temple continually praising God?

My (Tim) son Calvin loves *The Lion, the Witch, and the Wardrobe*. At the height of the final battle scene, when Peter and the White Witch duel for the soul of Narnia, all looks lost. Peter's army is beaten and fleeing; Peter himself is slowly giving ground to the witch. Slowly because the witch cruelly wants Peter to feel every humiliating blow to the fullest. As she is about to put an end to the charade, she is arrested by the sound of Aslan's roar. Turning to see Aslan standing on a nearby hillock, the witch whispers, "Impossible!" The last time Calvin watched the movie, he stood up at this point, shook his fist at the TV, and shouted, "POSSIBLE!"

That's how we should read Luke's "Amen." It's not some sort of pious intonation or religious formality. It is Luke's own joy spilling into his own story. It is his bridging of the narrative world and his own. Were we the writers, we might say, "It's true!" or "I agree!" or "Yes!" Even a fist pump would not be out of place.

Calvin's "POSSIBLE!" captures the essence of Luke's "Amen." The story of the victory of Jesus, like the story of the victory of Aslan, is very nearly an impossible story. It's almost too good to be true. But Luke's "Amen" is his declaration that he has staked his life on its truth, and it is his invitation to us to believe with him, and his proclamation that signs of its truth are all around us.

Now the danger of ascension living becomes clear. Jesus crowned means Jesus absent. But Jesus crowned means Jesus reigns. Now all earthly kings and princes find their own rule radically relativized. What if they do not acknowledge Jesus? To whom do Christians point when their allegiance is challenged? Because it lacks the faith of the writer to Hebrews, the world does not see Jesus. Christians now know that the powers—whether from Washington or New York or Moscow or Beijing or Mumbai—reign as part of an order that is passing away; an order that must finally yield before the true king. But what if these powers do not? The disciples could return to Jerusalem without fear, but can we? Ascension living is more immediately dangerous for some than others.

Let us all draw courage and direction from the Ascension! The absent Jesus shapes us to know that our courage comes not from ourselves, but from the Spirit of Jesus! The Spirit of Jesus—who emboldened Jesus to side with the poor and oppressed and identify with the outcasts to the point of death—emboldens us. The challenge to the powers of this earth is that while they may not see Jesus, if we wait for the power of the Spirit, they will see Jesus in us.

Perhaps there is more to this waiting than we care to admit. What reflection shaped the disciples in that waiting? What good but misdirected aims and hopes were shattered as they reflected on Jesus? Why do we not hear about the disciples' families, or businesses, or personal advancement in the Acts of the Apostles? Had these issues become secondary for the disciples?

Waiting for the Spirit reminds us that perhaps our aims and hopes still do not quite line up with the Jesus who is ascended.

Indeed, the Ascension is not simply a pronouncement on the powers and principalities of this earth, but on us, as well. Our lives and ambitions sit judged by the Cross and the reign of Jesus.

The Ascension, after all, is not only about the *reign* of Jesus, it is the reign of *Jesus*. That is, the absence of the one who was crucified means precisely that it is the crucified one—a real person—who is now reigning. "The Jesus who suffered and died is the same who is carried up into heaven to exercise royal power."

Thus, the Ascension's deconstruction of our spiritual lives can now take many forms: What in our requests to God—our requests for blessing, healing, opportunity, happiness—reflect the life of *this* first-century Jew? What on our prayer lists reflects a need for the courage that the disciples received with the Holy Spirit? Do we really need *any* courage in how *we* live out the Christian faith? If not, are we following the *ascended* Jesus?

This deconstruction can take ecclesial forms, as well. What resources do our churches seek—buildings, funds, computers, buses, sound equipment—and how do they reflect and further the aims of Jesus of Nazareth? The Ascension drives us back to waiting, reconsidering the life of the Jew who was crucified. The Ascension reworks the world from the ground up, and it does the same with our personal and corporate constructions of the Christian faith.

If Jesus reigns over *the world*, then everything is theological and open to ascension-deconstruction. Thus, the questions in the previous paragraph are not to condemn, but allow our lives to be molded by the narrative. And once molded, then our lives are free to enjoy the worship, blessing, and rejoicing the disciples experienced because their Lord ascended.

DISCUSSION QUESTIONS

1. Jesus is both absent and present. Which of these do you feel most strongly? At what times?

2. "Luke wants us to comprehend the coming of the Spirit as the earthly echo of the heavenly enthronement of the victorious Son." How might we think of Pentecost if it is so closely related to the Ascension?

3. The ascended Jesus deconstructs our prayer requests. Do you believe that prayers should be engaged so critically?

4. In what ways could deconstruction be a healthy practice in your life? In what ways could it be unhealthy?

5. How would you deconstruct elements of this book in light of the Ascension?

The Ascension
and the Christian Life

CONFESSION

THE ASCENSION AND THE POWERS

And after eight days again his disciples were within, and Thomas was with them: *then* came Jesus, the doors being shut, and stood in the midst, and said, Peace be unto you. Then saith he to Thomas, Reach hither thy finger, and behold my hands; and reach hither thy hand, and thrust it into my side and be not faithless, but believing. And Thomas answered and said unto him, My Lord and my God.

—The Gospel of John (20:26–28 KJV)

He showed them that after his resurrection his body was both incorruptible and yet could be touched. . . . By showing us that it is incorruptible, he would urge us on toward our reward, and by offering it as touchable he would dispose us toward faith. He manifested himself as both incorruptible and touchable to show us that his body after his resurrection was of the same nature as ours but of a different glory.

—Gregory the Great

Confession, says the cliché, is good for the soul. No doubt when this truism is trotted out, we have in mind the idea of unburdening ourselves of some secret sin. But what about another kind of confession? What about confessing our faith in the Creed? And specifically, what about saying, "I believe . . . He ascended into heaven?" Is that good for the soul, too?

Through the biblical confessions of Thomas and Stephen, we will explore the ethical implications of confession generally, and then in more detail, confession of the Ascension.

So, what does it mean to confess? Some churches confess a lot. The Apostles' or the Nicene Creed is confessed every Sunday. If this is your practice, have you ever attended to the language used? When we say, "I believe in God the Father, the Almighty . . ." or "I believe in Jesus Christ, his only Son our Lord . . ." what's going on? When we confess that "He ascended into heaven and is seated at the right hand of the Father . . ." what are we saying?

If we don't belong to a creedal church or participate in a similar liturgy on Sundays, we are not off the hook. All of us ought to weigh from time to time just what we are doing when we, with Thomas, confess that the ascended Jesus is Lord and God. All of us ought to consider what we are doing when we say, "I believe."

Most people, we suspect, would cast the act of confession in an epistemological light. When we say, "I believe," we are saying something such as "I believe it is true that. . . ." This is certainly what it means to believe in modern English. Belief has something to do with knowledge. It is poised on the knowledge scale somewhere between doubt and certainty.

So, when we confess the Creed, we are expressing our conviction that its contents are true. We believe that God exists, that God created all that is, that God took flesh in Jesus of Nazareth, that Jesus ascended in the flesh into heaven. We also believe that the United States is a country and that the Boston Bruins are a professional hockey team. We are saying that these things are true.

When it comes to confession, and certainly when it comes to confessing the Creed, this understanding of belief is basic, even assumed. But if we think that's all that is going on, we're wrong. There's much more to this than the recitation of a spiritual grocery list of facts.

For when we say, "I believe," we are also asserting that this story of God is God's one true story. We are saying the same thing as Jews when they pray the Shema from the book of Deuteronomy: "Hear, O Israel, the Lord is our God, the Lord alone" (6:4). The Lord that Jews confess, is the only God there is, and thereby they practice their identity as Jews. When Christians confess the Creed, we are saying that all other stories of God are at best, partial and at worst, false. The story crystallized in the Creed is *the story* of God and the world, and its confession is practicing the identity that story offers.

The Creed, in other words, is not a series of assertions to be fit into another worldview, or even shorthand for the worldview into which we fit everything else, but shapes its speakers in its worldview through repetition that provides new language.

The words "I believe" functioned in ancient Christian worship as *performatives*. That is to say, the words did something. Uttering them altered the speaker's situation. One analogy is the wedding vow. What seals a couple's marriage is the vows they take, spoken aloud to each other. Whoever presides—whether a religious representative or a justice of the peace—merely *pronounces* that a wedding has in fact taken place and can now be duly registered. Before vows are said, the couple are engaged; after the vows, they are married.

Another example is the apology that takes place with the expression, "I'm sorry." Sorrow may precede the words, but the apology requires verbalization. Situations change because words are spoken.

When Christians confess the Creed, when we say, "I believe," we are performing in a similar way. The confession is a pledge of life and a practice of this pledge to the one who ascended, body and soul, into heaven and is seated at the right hand of the Father. To confess those words is to pledge our troth—our loyalty—to the one of whom we speak and to practice the identity these words offer. Just as an appropriate "I love you" *expresses* love and loyalty, so does it *practice* the love that may have existed in one lover for another, yet remained hidden without expression.

What about confessing the Ascension, then? How does this confession itself shape us? The Johannine location and nature of Thomas' confession that Jesus is Lord and God can help us answer that question.

The words are easy to say, we might think, but much harder to live. We can say words, but, if we practice the identity found therein only verbally, and are not shaped by them, what's the value? This imperfection reflects a current popular state of religious practice that splits body from soul, private from public. To this split the Ascension puts the lie.

A conversation between me (Tim) and one of my students illustrates this supposed distinction. "Dr. Perry, can I ask you something, um, personal?" The student shifted uncomfortably in her chair. Forming college and seminary students spiritually and academically is a significant aspect of the Christian's academic vocation, and this often leads to in-depth conversations, yet one is never at ease when a conversation begins with this question.

The conversations that follow this question can take any number of directions. The conversation could be about family life or personal devotional practice. It could be about suffering—real suffering—in the student's life who has just encountered disease and death for the first time and is existentially unsatisfied with the various available explanations. Sometimes the conversation could be about something completely different.

This conversation turned out to be one of the last kind. The student launched in: "Should I get a tattoo or not 'cause all my friends have one, but my dad says I shouldn't 'cause the Bible says I can't, and he says that I should talk to a professor if I don't believe him." Imagine that speech delivered with all the care and sensitivity of a Gatling gun.

Clearly, this student was searching for ammunition in a family argument. Any attempt to nuance her father's reading of the Bible would be interpreted as giving permission; any expression of caution—"You know, maybe your father has a point"—would in all likelihood have ended the talk prematurely. So, after a quick wordless prayer for wisdom, I asked the student a question. "I'll answer you if you will answer a question for me first. Why do you want to mark your body?"

"It's not like anybody's going to see it."

"OK. Fair enough. I don't care where it goes. I just want to know why you want to mark your body."

"I dunno. 'Cause it's my body and I want to."

Unfortunately, a helpful discussion around what it means to be made in God's image, to be gradually conformed to the image of Christ, around how to understand that he was *marked* for us in his suffering, we are *marked* by Christ in baptism, and whether any of these issues change how we might think about tattoos, did not develop.

Beneath the tattoo debate, profound, ultimately theological issues about identity, and whether it is constructed or received, lay awaiting exposure and debate. Consider, again, the student's declaration: " 'Cause it's my body and I want to."

This statement illustrates the presumed public from private, fact from value distinction. In this case, the division was expressed as self (or perhaps, soul) and body. Perhaps this student believed that faith is inner, private. Faith is spiritual and spiritual means immaterial, having nothing to do with our bodies and what we do with them. Our bodies, in this way of thinking, become basically instrumental. We "do" things with them. They do not constitute our selves. Rather, they are at our disposal as just one more means of self-expression.

In this way of thinking, Jesus makes no necessary claims on our visible selves, but only on our invisible souls. This takes an ascension-never-happened approach to life because

Jesus rose *in his body* and he ascended *in this same body*. When he appeared to Thomas and the rest of the disciples one week after Easter, he displayed the wounds in his body. And the display of those wounds prompted Thomas' confession. Jesus' ascension was not his departure from his body; *it was his body-and-soul enthronement in heaven*. John tells us that the Word was made flesh and the Ascension tells us that the Word will always be flesh—wounded flesh. John wants us to see that this has to do with our confessions, our pledges of allegiances, and our practice of them.

Of course, my student wasn't thinking this through explicitly. She was not a conscious "Gnostic," denying the materiality of our Lord's incarnation and its impact upon our material bodies.

In all likelihood, the student would have offered orthodox, specifically evangelical responses to specific doctrinal questions. But that's precisely the point. The problem wasn't her answer, but that her answer wasn't integrated with her practice of Jesus as Lord. She had split confession from practice.

This split seems part of the cultural air we breathe. We are encouraged to make faith a private matter. We are expected to divorce faith from daily, public practices. We fail to see this disintegration as problematic. As we navigate the challenges of life, there is pressure to keep dorm separate from class, home from school, and friends from colleagues.

At just this point Christian counterculture begins, and the Ascension can shape us accordingly. When he ascended, Jesus went into his Father's presence to receive his kingdom. When he sat down at God's right hand, he began to rule over his enemies. He challenges the principalities and powers and even the "gods" that lie behind the misuse of political authority. For Jesus and his followers, the Ascension is a public matter, a public confrontation between Jesus and the spiritual powers and the public victory of Jesus over those powers.

This is made clear in the Ascension confession of Thomas. The story of Thomas' confession starts like this:

> Thomas . . . was not with them when Jesus came. So the other disciples told him, "We have seen the Lord." But he said to them, "Unless I see the mark of the nails in his hands, and put my finger in the mark of the nails and my hand in his side, I will not believe."
>
> A week later, his disciples were again in the house, and Thomas was with them. Although the doors were shut, Jesus came and stood among them and said, "Peace be with you." Then he said to Thomas, "Put your finger here and see my hands. Reach out your hand and put it in my side. Do not doubt but believe." Thomas answered him, "My Lord and my God!" Jesus said to him, "Have you believed because you have seen me? Blessed are those who have not seen and yet have come to believe" (John 20:24–29).

We find the disciples huddled in a house, the doors shut and locked. The disciples had already heard Mary Magdalene's report that Jesus was alive. They had even seen Jesus themselves one week earlier. On the first day of the week, when the disciples were terrified that the wrath that had been poured out upon Jesus would also be visited upon them, they were hiding out in a house—shivering behind dead-bolted doors.

And Jesus appeared to them.

He spoke words of peace to them. He showed them his wounds. And when he departed, we read that the disciples were glad.

One week later, though, the doors are once more locked. Presumably the fear that had prompted their locking them on the first day had not abated entirely. Well, who can blame the disciples? Resurrections are not everyday occurrences and those who killed Jesus would still have wanted to snuff out any signs of a following.

For whatever reason, the second Sunday evening starts much as the first. Huddled around some small oil lamps, the disciples whisper and wonder. This time, Thomas is with them.

John is quick to tell us that it is the eighth day. On one level, he offers a straightforward announcement of the time. On the Jewish way of reckoning, it is one week later: the Sunday after the first Easter Sunday. One week after Mary Magdalene, the apostle to the apostles, was greeted with the strange command, "Stop clinging to Me, for I have not yet ascended to the Father," and equally strange commission "Go to My brethren and say to them, 'I ascend to My Father and to your Father.'" (John 20:17 NAS). One week after the ascending Jesus appeared to the disciples, breathed his Spirit into them, and commissioned them for the ministry of the forgiveness of sins.

But of course, John is never content with straightforward announcements. There's more going on here. It is the eighth day. The day of new beginnings. The day of the victory of the Living One. The day of celebration. The Lord's Day. For

John, as for the early Christians, every Sunday, every eighth day, was a miniature Easter. The *Epistle of Barnabas*, written around the same time as the fourth Gospel, says "we keep the eighth day for rejoicing, [when] Jesus rose from the dead, and having been manifested ascended into the heavens." These words capture the spirit that infuses our celebrations that continue to take place on the eighth day.

It was the eighth day. In announcing the time in this way, John implicitly rebukes the locked-door disciples. Jesus had risen. The Holy Spirit had been given. And the doors, on the eighth day of all days, should have been flung wide open. But they weren't. They were keeping private their previously public fellowship.

On this eighth day, we meet Thomas, who was not with the rest when the ascending Lord appeared to them in the locked room one week before. We call him "Doubting Thomas" for the height at which he sets the bar for his assent to the disciples' report: "Unless I see the mark of the nails in his hands, and put my finger in the mark of the nails and my hand in his side, I will not believe." A high bar to be sure. But is it fair to add *doubting* to his name? Mary and the other disciples had had a physical encounter with Jesus—Mary had even laid hold of him; he displayed his wounded hands and side to the rest. This was no ghost. Jesus had hinged thumbs and toes and pumping heart and windswept hair—materiality. Was it unfair for Thomas to desire the same knowledge of Jesus as the other disciples had?

When we look at Thomas' description elsewhere in the Gospel, the word "doubting" is never appropriate. Thomas grasps the provocative nature of Jesus' commitment to go back to Jerusalem to face the wrath of the Jewish religious leadership, saying, "Let us also go, that we may die with him" (John 11:16b). Thomas understands that the sojourn from Lazarus' tomb outside Bethany will end at Jesus' own tomb outside Jerusalem. Thomas knows that Jesus is a "dead man walking." And Thomas resolves to go to Jerusalem anyway. He is *loyal* Thomas.

Thomas alone of the disciples confesses his and his fellow apostles' ignorance of Jesus' ultimate destination: "Lord, we do not know where you are going. How can we know the way?" (John 14:5). Thomas wants to know the way to go. He is *honest* Thomas.

And loyal, honest Thomas because he is loyal and honest wants to see the wounds. He wants to know in as full a way as Mary—as full a way as Peter—as full a way as Philip. He wants to know that the hour when his Lord was lifted up on the cross was the hour of his exaltation. The hour when the glory of the only Son of the Father was displayed to those who had eyes to see and ears to hear.

This is no skeptic, no atheist, no cynic daring the disciples to make him believe. "Unless I see the wounds. Unless I touch him"—these are the words of a wounded lover who dared not hope against the awful weight of the reality of death that there was an ember left in the midst of the ashes of his loyalty.

It is loyal Thomas, honest Thomas who has come, one week after the Resurrection, on the eighth day, into the house with the other disciples, and the doors were shut. Loyal Thomas, honest Thomas *confesses the ascension truth*: "My Lord and my God!"

Thomas' confession of the identity of Jesus as Lord and God is an oath. For if the wounded Jesus is the one true Lord and God, then there could be no competitors for Thomas' loyalty. "For even if there are so-called gods whether in heaven or on earth, as indeed there are many gods and many lords, yet for us there is but one God, the Father, from whom are all things and we exist for Him; and one Lord, Jesus Christ, by whom are all things, and we exist through Him," wrote Paul (1 Corinthians 8:5–6 NAS). But these words also express what is so pithily confessed in Thomas' five words. There is one Lord Jesus Christ before whom all other lords and gods must eventually bow.

"Lord and God" may well have been an echo of the reign of the Emperor Domitian, who reigned from 81 to 96, when the Gospel of John was written. Tradition has it that his violence was second only to Nero. And even skeptical scholars agree that Domitian could be ruthless when presented with opposition or ambition. Historians have also noticed how he uniquely signed his decrees with the words, *"Dominus et deus noster"* (Our Lord and God).

Apparently he was especially fond of taking the title when he signed decrees of execution: "It has pleased our Lord and God to require your life." John's readers would have known full well the depth of Thomas' words. Another Lord and God had claimed him. Another Lord and God had required his life. Another Lord and God had claimed John's first readers, too. Whatever Caesar could require, the confession of Caesar as Lord and God would never come from an early believer. Caesar's authority extended only to the body. Thomas' Lord and God invited the fealty of both body and soul.

Thomas' ascension-confession is his public oath of allegiance to Jesus and to none other. The public reading of the Gospel of John, including Thomas' confession, at Christian gatherings throughout ancient Ephesus would have amounted to the same thing. The disciples were keeping the faith private; Thomas makes it public. The personal pronouns give Thomas' words even more weight. *My* lord and *my* God. He declares his *personal* allegiance publicly.

Confession of all stripes makes public what is private. It takes what is inside and makes it available to a select group. Thus, there is no significant difference between unburdening souls and confessing Creeds. They are both enactments of making public what we may be tempted to keep private. The Ascension's public claim, made clear by the words of Thomas, reinforces how confessing itself is a practice of the Ascension.

In what manner can our public confessions of faith reveal our allegiance to Jesus as king? If we allow the confession to shape us, then our public words must also be words of fealty to Jesus; otherwise, we have not learned from the confession of Thomas. Our challenge is to make our confession also our practice.

The story of Thomas' ascension confession also shapes us in another way. Thomas' challenge was in seeing Jesus the way the other disciples had seen him. The great American novelist John Updike captured the depth of Thomas' conviction in the opening words of his famous poem "Seven Stanzas at Easter:"

> Make no mistake: if He rose at all
> it was as his body.

Listen to Jesus' words to Thomas on the eighth day: "Put your finger here and see my hands. Reach out your hand and put it in my side" (John 20:27). The one who was crucified has now been revealed as Lord and God. He was crucified in his body. His divine nature did not abandon his human body. He who hung the stars in place now hung on the cross in his humanity, in his body. He suffered in his humanity, in his body. He died in his humanity, in his body. He was raised in his humanity, in his body. He ascended in his humanity, in his body. It is in his humanity, in his wound-bearing body that he presents himself to his Father.

"The only begotten Word of God ascended into the heavens with his flesh united to him," writes Cyril of Alexandria. Cyril's point is to underscore how the resurrection and ascension of Jesus are to be understood in relation to his crucifixion.

Athanasius wrote that "he became as we are in order that we might become as he is," and he has not ceased to be like us. To quote Peter Widdicombe, "The divine one, equal to the Father, who went down has suffered and died as a man in the body and that very same man in the very same body, replete with evidence of his death for humankind has gone up."

The wounds of Jesus displayed to Thomas are signs of the deep truth of the Ascension: that God has come to us as one of us and where we would fight and fail, he has fought and conquered. The wounds are thus no longer signs of his humiliation. They are, in the words of Matthew Bridges's hymn, *Crown Him with Many Crowns* "rich wounds yet visible above in beauty glorified."

And we are drawn by Thomas' words back to the prologue of this marvelous telling of the Good News: "And the Word became flesh and lived among us, and we have seen his glory, the glory as of a father's only son, full of grace and truth" (John 1:14). It has taken a long time—three or perhaps four years—but at last, the disciples, with Thomas in the lead, see the glory of God's one and only—the glory that was his before the creation of the world. And it is the glory revealed in a body wounded and alive again, and ascending to the Father, even as the disciples encounter it behind locked doors.

The Word was made flesh and the Word never ceased being flesh, even bearing wounds received in his flesh. John tells us that everything was made through the Word and, because of the bodily ascension, we know the Word continues making, even in the flesh. As such, we know that our words do not only *do*, but *make* in ways that reflect Jesus. This ascension lesson is well primed for the postmodern world: language shapes reality. Enfleshed language, says the Ascension, shapes our world. As such, confessing the Creed shapes how we interpret the world in which we live.

The Ascension through the words of Thomas recaptures the practice of language for us today. We do well to reexamine the language we teach and learn in Sunday worship.

The following story illustrates how this issue has personal implications for me (Tim). My friend David is a priest who became an academic; I am an academic recently ordained. Our mirrored vocational journeys have facilitated long conversations. On one occasion, David questioned whether I would wear the clerical collar in the classroom. My reaction was that I would not, because the classroom was not the place for a collar—the church was. Being about pastoral work in the parish occasioned the collar. Yet was I succumbing to the same public-private, faith-fact façade?

David was able to see through this error. "If you're a priest, you're a priest all the time. And you wear the marks of your office." David was right to affirm that the classroom is the most important place to wear the collar, perhaps more than the church sanctuary. For in so doing, the public-private distinction is *contradicted* in a profound way. The collar in the classroom affirms that matters of faith and fact are so deeply interwoven as to be inseparable. The very public-private distinction upon which so much of modern life is dependent functions at the level of a *religious* assumption. The collar, among other things, is the mark of the priestly office. It doesn't tell people what the priest does; it tells them who and whose the priest is.

Priests wear the marks of the office in public because the ascended Jesus continues to bear the marks of his office in public—in his hands, feet, and side and on his brow. He bears them all the time as part of his glorified body. He can no more put them off than he can put off that body. For they are the signs that the crucified one has triumphed over death; that the risen one is he who was crucified; that the ascended one reigns as precisely as the one who suffered.

Mel Gibson's *The Passion of the Christ* continues to be a lightning rod for controversy both within and outside Christian communities, as it still profoundly moves and disturbs believers and nonbelievers alike. It assaults the senses intentionally—even to the very end. Indeed, the movie's concluding scene is the most powerful of the film.

In this brief segment, the stone rolls away. Sunlight streams into the tomb. A naked and very much alive Jesus walks out. As he does, the camera focuses on his hand. And through the hole in his hand, we can see the hairs on his thigh. Whatever we might think of Gibson and his movie, surely in this instance he gets his theology of the body exactly right. The glory of God, the sum of God's attributes, God's very identity is revealed in this very wounded, very human body made alive. He displays his marks—forever.

This one who suffered, and no other, is Lord and God. This one and no other is the glory of the Father full of grace and truth. This one and no other has come down. This one and no other has suffered and died. This one and no other rose again. This one and no other has gone up. This one and no other reigns. This fleshly, material, bodily way is the way the Word reveals his glory. Having ascended to the Father, he is *the way* to the Father. The crucified and risen one is the Lord who is God.

What marks do we bear that resemble this one? What visible marks? What invisible marks? Could this provide the avenue in which baptism, even infant baptism, could be understood in a culture with its increasing obsession of being marked? Could this avenue provide theological grounding and language for the powerful "To Write Love on Her Arms" project, which ministers to "cutters," those who desire to mark their bodies in destructive ways?

Jesus' body has been marked for us. And as a result, our bodies are not our own. We are not our own. We belong to another. His risen, ascended body bears the signs of his saving work, to show us that he has claimed us as his own.

If we are his, in some sense, his marks—the marks of his suffering and death—are also to be our marks. In our baptism, we have put on Christ-with-his-wounds. There is no other Christ to put on. Thomas *confessed* and *practiced* this. And so must we.

DISCUSSION QUESTIONS

1. How can you identify with Thomas?
2. Do you see a connection between confession as recitation of creed and confession as baring one's soul because both are formative? Do you agree that speech can be so formative?
3. Where do you see the public-private division at work in your community or church?
4. Do you agree about the importance of Jesus' scars in developing a theology of the body? Why or why not?

6

MARTYRDOM

THE END OF WITNESS

But [Stephen], being full of the Holy Ghost, looked up stedfastly into heaven, and saw the glory of God, and Jesus standing on the right hand of God, And said, Behold, I see the heavens opened, and the Son of man standing at the right hand of God. Then they cried out with a loud voice, and stopped their ears, and ran upon him with one accord, And cast him out of the city, and stoned him. . . .

—The Acts of the Apostles (7:55–58 KJV)

But as in the persecutions which happen from time to time, so also then God will permit these things, not because He wants power to hinder them, but because according to His wont He will through patience crown His own champions like as He did His Prophets and Apostles; to the end that having toiled for a little while they may inherit the eternal kingdom of heaven.

—Cyril of Jerusalem (adapted)

The world is not growing more and more secular. Precisely the opposite is happening: our world is becoming more and more religious. Look at the evidence: In Russia, the Orthodox Church is making an unprecedented comeback after the Soviet era. In India, the world's largest democracy's Bharatiya Janata Party (BJP) is actively, sometimes militantly, Hindu. In China, there are more Christians than there are official members of the Communist Party. The numbers of Christians and Muslims in sub-Saharan Africa are growing and causing religious tensions in countries such as Nigeria and Kenya. Even in Europe, the same immigration policies that have led to expanding Muslim minorities are, as Philip Jenkins observes in *God's Continent*, solidifying European Christianity in various, often nontraditional, forms. Of course, such overt religious expression need not be so formal: violence perpetrated in loyalty to sports teams and the identity-centered advertisements of MAC vs. PC reveal a religious nature.

As the world becomes more religious, it is also coming more and more to resemble the world in which the first Christians lived. This world, defined by the might of the Roman Empire, was a world in which many religious narratives vied with each other for their adherents' loyalty. All the while, Rome kept the peace through its military power. Religions such as Gnosticism and the mystery religions of Osiris and Mithras were tolerated only because their claims did not conflict with the reign of Rome. Jews made public claims about their God, claims for loyalty, but were focused on their own land and temple. They would be tolerated too, so long as they didn't make trouble.

On the one hand, as with their pagan contemporaries, early Christians invited everyone to join them, regardless of race or geography. On the other hand, like their Jewish brothers and sisters, they made public claims about the nature of God and God's reign. Early Christians and the powers of their day understood Thomas' confession to be a direct challenge to Caesar's own claims to authority. They understood Paul's challenge that citizenship with Christ in heaven competed with Roman citizenship. If Jesus had ascended and had taken his throne as Lord and God, then even Caesar would one day bow the knee to him. Christians swore primary allegiance to Christ.

Early Christian apologists—both in the pages of the New Testament and outside it—understood how the claims of primary allegiance to Christ relativized all other loyalties. These writers asserted that because Christians bowed the knee to Jesus, they would pray for the well-being of the Emperor (Peter); that Christians would even acknowledge Caesar's reign as divinely instituted (Paul); that what Christians revered in Jesus was the completion of the highest and best of pagan philosophy (Justin Martyr). Far from being revolutionaries, these early Christians tried to present themselves as model citizens.

In a world becoming more and more religious, with conflicting loyalties in multiple spheres, Christians must learn how to navigate the same rough waters as their spiritual ancestors did. Early Christians tried to navigate these tensions, with appeals to the governing authorities—"apologies"—for their way of life. Sometimes such defenses worked; often they did not. So, alongside the growth of "apologies" in early Christian literature, there also grew "martyrologies." Christians not only defended their way of life to the secular powers, they recalled and celebrated the way to death of their greatest witnesses—their martyrs. So popular did this genre become that its greatest stories—Polycarp of Smyrna, Lawrence, Agnes, along with many others—were widely copied and circulated in the ancient world and as a result can still be read today. These accounts reflected the route taken when conflicting allegiances were brought to the highest stakes.

So, where should we go in a time such as this—a time of increasing religiosity, increasing demands for loyalty? To Polycarp, Lawrence, Agnes? Yes! And also to the other witnesses, ancient and modern, who testified to the reign of Jesus by the relinquishing of their lives. First, however, we will turn to the Bible, and to the story of Stephen the protomartyr, the first to witness to the reign of Jesus by identifying with Jesus in his death. But our story starts before these martyrs. It starts before the first Christian martyr, though his story, shaped by the Ascension, provides the greatest opportunity for the reflection. It starts with the Acts of the Apostles, just after the Lord ascended.

> Jesus had warned his disciples to expect that his enemies would soon come after his followers. They "will arrest you and persecute you; they will hand you over to synagogues and prisons, and you will be brought before kings and governors because of my name. This will give you an opportunity to testify. So make up your minds not to prepare your defense in advance; for I will give you words and a wisdom that none of your opponents will be able to withstand or contradict. . . . By your endurance you will gain your souls. (Luke 21:12–15, 19)

In fulfillment of Jesus' words, Peter and John had answered for the "crime" of healing a crippled beggar in the name of Jesus outside the temple courtyard. At that time, Peter announced that God had raised Jesus of Nazareth from the dead and exalted him. Now, salvation—healing for both body and soul—could be found in no other name. Afraid of the crowd that was praising God for the miracle, the Council let Peter and John go.

However, the situation escalated. After yet more healings in Jesus' name, the apostles were rounded up and jailed. Peter, being summoned a second time, again spoke for the company. His sermon in brief: God raised and exalted Jesus of Nazareth to reign; we have seen it; we cannot keep silent about it; we must obey God more than human authorities (Acts 5:29–32).

Had a wise old Pharisee named Gamaliel not urged caution, the apostles would have been martyred on the spot (Acts 5:33–40). Instead, they were beaten, told to keep quiet, and sent home. Once home though, they preached all the more, rejoicing, Luke says, that "they were considered worthy to suffer dishonor for the sake of the name" (Acts 5:41).

The disciples' preaching was public and was grounded directly and deliberately in the public exaltation—the ascension of Jesus to God's right hand. Jesus' reign belayed the Council's commands. When faced with a conflict—the ascended Lord's commission to announce the Good News against the Council's command to shut up—the disciples obeyed Jesus and joyfully embraced the consequences. Jesus' ascension determined the disciples' actions.

It is essential to note that although the disciples are seemingly driven by persecution to fulfill the Great Commission, the conflict is never presented as *necessary or inevitable.* Thus Peter and John say to the Council in Acts 5, they must obey God "more than" the Council. The Greek word is *mallon*—and is often mistranslated as "rather than" or "instead of." There is no necessary conflict between earthly rule and Jesus' rule. There is no necessary conflict between the word of the Council and the Word of the ascended Lord. And yet, when confronted with the conflicting claims of earthly and heavenly crowns, the disciples opt for the crown of thorns, rejoicing that they have been counted worthy to suffer as their Lord once did. Loyalty to Christ, precisely because of his ascension, supersedes all other loyalties—including political and national loyalties.

The narrative of Acts, however, does not tell of ordered loyalties living in harmony. Instead, there is a clear escalation in the conflict between the disciples and the Jewish leadership in Jerusalem. Warning, then flogging—what's next? The growing tension in the first two accounts prepares us for the third: Stephen has been called to account for healing the sick and confounding debaters in the Synagogue of Freedmen.

Stephen was officially a deacon—set apart to care for the physical needs of the early Christian community. Yet more than a parish administrator, he was an evangelist and apologist. Stephen proclaimed and defended the truth of the reign of Jesus in local synagogues. Such was his eloquence that he aroused powerful opposition and was hauled before the very same court that had tried Jesus.

When Stephen is called to give his account, the apostles knew that this situation was different because false witnesses were used to charge Stephen with speaking blasphemy, decrying the temple, and saying that Jesus would destroy it. Peter especially would have remembered that the same charges had been brought against Jesus, and he likely had an inkling of how this would end. "By your endurance," Jesus said, "you will gain your souls" (Luke 21:19). As the apostles rushed to the Council chamber, Jesus' warning echoed in their ears.

Stephen is brought before the high priest and the Council and the young deacon is asked to answer the charges set against him: "Are these things so?" intones Caiaphas. "Answer, Stephen. The same charges brought against the one you call Lord are now laid at your feet."

The Holy Spirit gives Stephen the words to defend his Lord and the way to which his Lord had called him. Stephen retells the narrative of God's travails with God's people and how they persistently rejected him even to the present day. In Stephen's eyes, the nation is aptly named Jacob. For the history of Israel is a history of struggling with God, of resisting his covenant, of disobeying his law, of persecuting his prophets. The murder of Jesus is the climax of a long story of God's spurned love for his people. Stephen's words transformed the Council into a mob. They hustled him out of the city and stoned him.

Outside the courtroom, as he is dying, Stephen speaks three more times. He announces a vision: "I see the heavens opened and the Son of Man standing at the right hand of God!" And he prays—for himself, "Lord Jesus, receive my spirit," and for his killers, "Lord, do not hold this sin against them" (Acts 7:56, 59, 60).

The earliest martyrologies after Stephen's death follow a simple formula: an opening description of the sanctity of the protagonist is followed by an unjust accusation made by a jealous non-Christian. After the arrest and mock trial, the sentence of death is passed. Miraculously, though, the early martyrs do not die quickly. They are at first impervious to blade, flame, and sexual humiliation, all the while proclaiming that because their hope lies in the Lord Jesus they are already safe from harm. Sometimes, their final words are tinged with notes of defiance. "Eighty and six years have I served him and he has done me no wrong." Polycarp is reported to have said to the magistrate presiding at his execution. "I will not fail him now."

Luke, however, presents the orchestrated murder of Stephen as parallel to the orchestrated murder of Jesus: placed in the same court; tried by the same judge; on the same charges; resulting in the same verdict. Now, as Stephen dies, the identification with Jesus is complete, down to the last words.

Each successive speech is modeled after those of Jesus' own words at his trial and execution. Stephen says, "I see the Son of Man standing. . . ." where Jesus says "I am; and 'you will see the Son of Man seated at the right hand of the Power,' and 'coming with the clouds of heaven'" (Mark 14:62). When Stephen prays, "Lord Jesus, receive my spirit," we hear the echo of Jesus' prayer "Father, into your hands I commend my spirit" (Luke 23:46). When Stephen intercedes for his killers, we recall Jesus' prayer: "Father, forgive them; for they do not know what they are doing" (Luke 23:34). Stephen's imitation of his Lord— Stephen's identification with Jesus in his suffering—is entire. In fulfillment of his Lord's words, Stephen has denied himself, taken up his cross, and followed to the very end.

At the same time, the speeches differ in significant ways. They differ precisely because of the Ascension. Jesus' final two prayers were prayers to his Father. Stephen's final two prayers were prayers to the *ascended Lord*.

Stephen is no less Jewish than Jesus. And yet, Stephen prays to Jesus—as the one who can and will receive him, as the one who can and will condemn or acquit sinners. Within a few years of Jesus' death, resurrection, and ascension, Jewish Christians—men and women who began every day with the recitation of the Shema, "Hear O Israel, the LORD is One!"—were offering prayers to Jesus.

Historian Jaroslav Pelikan puts it provocatively: "[F]or Stephen to commit his spirit to the Lord Jesus . . . was either an act of blatant idolatry or the acknowledgment of the [Lord Jesus] as the fitting recipient of the dying prayer of Stephen.

The question Pelikan asks but doesn't answer, though, is this: how did Stephen know that the Lord Jesus was in fact able to receive his prayer? What led him to understand that the Lord Jesus was able to receive prayers and forgive sins—things only God could do?

The answer is found in Stephen's first speech and to a significant change in stance. Where Jesus said, "You shall see the Son of Man sitting," Stephen said, "I see the Son of Man standing." Why is the Lord standing?

The allusion to the Son of Man seated at the right hand of God is frequently used in the New Testament to describe the ascension and reign of Jesus. It is a reference to Psalm 110:1, "The Lord says to my Lord, sit at my right hand until I make your enemies your footstool." And whenever the allusion is made, Jesus—the ascended Lord—is *always* portrayed as sitting. Remember the language of Hebrews: "When he had made purification for sins, he sat down" (1:3).

Sitting is important. Sitting means both the completion of Christ's earthly, atoning work and the beginning of his heavenly reign. Here, as Stephen's face shone like that of an angel and the stones fell, the ascended Jesus stands. Since sitting is so significant, Jesus' standing cannot be a slip of Luke's imagination. Jesus stands for a reason.

Perhaps Jesus stands in response to Stephen's prayer to receive his spirit. Jesus stands to receive him, to welcome his first martyr, and to offer to him the victor's crown. This is an athletic image common to the ancient world in which Luke lived and Stephen died. It's not the only possibility. What if the ascended Lord rises to pass judgment on the crimes now taking place? Again in response to Stephen's prayers Jesus stands—this time to acquit Stephen's killers. Neither reading excludes the other; both hinge on the content of Stephen's prayers.

We find a third reading compelling: the ascended one stands neither to receive Stephen nor to judge his executioners, but to identify with Stephen. If the first readings focus on the specifics of Stephen's speeches, this one draws on the theme of identification. All the way through, Luke constructs his story to show Stephen's full identification with his Lord. Now, at the end there is a twist: the Lord stands to show *his* full identification with Stephen.

Prior to his ascension, Jesus had promised that "[e]veryone who acknowledges me before others, the Son of Man also will acknowledge before the angels of God" (Luke 12:8). Now having received his kingdom, Jesus makes good on his word. He stands to vindicate before his angels and his Father his witness, Stephen. He stands in effect to say to the heavenly court, "He's with me. I am for him."

Here's where we enter Stephen's story: the same ascension call is laid upon us. If we have followed Thomas in his confession of the ascended Lord as "My Lord and my God," then there is no room for *final loyalty* to those whom Paul calls the "many lords" and "many gods" that run our day-to-day lives. And it is inevitable, in our increasingly religious-political world, that such loyalties will be tested. It is inevitable that we will be called to give a public accounting of what Peter calls "the hope that is within us."

With Peter, Paul, and the early apologists such as Justin Martyr, we find ourselves praying for those who govern our lives, recognizing that their rule is in some way instituted by God. Christians are good citizens. A life shaped by a deep awareness of the ascension of Jesus, prays for peace in cities in which we are not fully at home. With Stephen and Augustine, we find ourselves insisting that this rule is at best penultimate and that our true allegiance lies elsewhere. For we have taken an oath of allegiance to another king and have become citizens of another country. We are only pilgrims.

So what does tiered political faithfulness look like? How do we concretize this concept and practice this principle?

Consider the believing citizen of a nation at war. Christians in the United States pray earnestly for American soldiers overseas, and the immediate and extended families of these soldiers. Tiered political faithfulness demands that these same Christians pray more earnestly for Christians in Iraq.

Do American citizens have a duty to pray for American soldiers? Most certainly. Origen writes that though Christians were not to fight with their hands, they were to "fight through their prayer to God on behalf of those doing battle in a just cause and on behalf of an emperor who is ruling justly."

But the Ascension also claims that the Christian's first loyalty is to Christ and to the people united in his lordship. Christians in America and Canada and Italy and Australia should be praying for the forces representing their nations, but first for their brothers and sisters in Christ living in whatever country. Moreover, the fervency with which prayers are offered for loved ones becomes a condemnation when our prayers lack in fervor for brothers and sisters in Christ we have not seen.

Yet perhaps the most expressive formative nature of Stephen's story regarding his loyalty to Jesus is his practice of forgiveness. As we saw earlier, the Ascension makes the cross a victory, and Jesus' words on the cross, "Father forgive them," reflect Stephen's words for God not to hold this sin against them. This means that part of Stephen's own victory in his conflicting allegiance is that he kept faithful—to God and to his oppressors.

Forgiveness as a positive act expresses one's commitment to relate properly with the oppressor. Of course such proper relationship becomes complex in a world of conflicting powers, and much abuse has gone under the banner of Christian calls to forgive and be restored, when unresolved sin still threatens violence against those called to forgive. Some forgiveness is only safe eschatologically.

The practice of forgiveness reveals, sometimes on multiple occasions, the opppresssor's disloyalty to the forgiver. The Cross of Christ is not only a victory, but a condemnation of Christ's oppressors because their disloyalty to an innocent man and his God is there revealed. Stephen's practice of forgiveness reveals his faithfulness to God and to his oppressors even while it reveals his oppressors' faithlessness and disloyalty. The ascension-shaped Christian, with tensions of loyalty, bravely practices forgiveness, even to the point of martyrdom, yet sees the ascended Jesus standing with him. The ascension-shaped life bears Jesus' promise, "by your endurance shall you gain your souls" and confesses with Stephen, "I see the Son of Man standing."

This chapter is best concluded with the narratives of two saints who died at the hands of disloyal oppressors, even while they exhibited appropriately tiered loyalty. Once, when he was preaching in Westminster Abbey in front of King Henry VIII, Anglican preacher Bishop Hugh Latimer reflected aloud in midsermon on the peculiar situation he faced: "Latimer! Latimer! Latimer! Be careful what you say! The King of England is here!" Then he continued, "Latimer! Latimer! Latimer! Be careful what you say! The King of kings is here!" Latimer testified before King Henry who, history records, could brook very little opposition, that his final allegiance was owed to another: King Jesus.

It is in part because of his conviction that loyalty to Christ trumped loyalty to Crown that Hugh Latimer is not remembered as a bishop and preacher of the English Reformation. Rather, he is remembered as one of the Oxford Martyrs burned at the stake during the reign of Henry's Catholic daughter, Mary Tudor.

Along with Latimer, St. Thomas More shared the awareness that loyalty to Christ came ahead of everything else. Thomas More was a humanist, scholar, and close advisor to King Henry VIII. When Henry proclaimed himself head of the church, however, More broke with him, all the while insisting on his loyalty to the Crown. He ended up in prison despite his best efforts and after a trial whose verdict rested on perjured testimony, More was sentenced to death by beheading. His last recorded words, uttered from the scaffold on July 6, 1535, were these: "I die the King's good servant *and* God's first."

These martyrdoms exemplify the story that tells us that Jesus reigns and that Jesus is ascended. These stories also tell us that Jesus is still standing.

DISCUSSION QUESTIONS

1. Do you agree that the language and practice of martyrdom must be recovered? Why or why not?
2. The authors believe that national allegiances must be subverted to spiritual allegiances and that these relationships may exist in harmony. How do you consider the relationship between national and spiritual relationships?
3. What other allegiance could conflict with spiritual allegiances?

7

SACRAMENT

THE PROMISE OF PRESENCE

And it came to pass, as he sat at meat with them, he took bread, and blessed it, and brake, and gave to them. And their eyes were opened, and they knew him; and he vanished out of their sight. And they said one to another, Did not our heart burn within us, while he talked with us by the way, and while he opened to us the scriptures?

—The Gospel of Luke (24:30–32 KJV)

Jesus stirred up their minds by the writings of the law and the prophets; He afterward more plainly sets Himself before them, when, having consented to their request to go with them to the village, He took bread, and blessed it, and brake, and divided it among them. *For their eyes*, it says, *were held that they might not know Him*, until namely the word had entered stirring up their heart unto faith and then, rendering what they had before heard and believed visible, He offered them the sight seasonably after the hearing. He does not, however, continue with them, for *He vanished*, it says, *out of their sight*. For our Lord's relation unto men after His resurrection does not continue the same as before.

—Cyril of Alexandria (adapted)

The Ascension holds the paradox of absence and presence. It is a paradox that shapes the way disciples live. We remember the Ascension and its meaning: Jesus reigns. And in the midst of our memory, we are also to look forward to the day when that reign will be publicly obvious. Looking back and ahead are both wrapped up in Jesus' words, "[L]ift up your heads, because your redemption is drawing near" (Luke 21:28 NAS).

Recognizing the reign of Jesus results in a confession—the ascended one is both Lord and God. His reign, in other words, is not confined to the private realm of spiritual experience. It is public. It shapes our lives in public ways. Even down to what we do with our bodies.

Jesus' rule is both mediated through, and in tension with, the reigns of all those whose decisions chart the courses of so much of our lives. There is no necessary conflict between Christ and Caesar. But Caesar will from time to time encroach upon the reign of the ascended Lord. In such times, by our endurance, the ascended one says, we will gain our souls— just like Stephen.

Now the final question: how does the paradoxical absence and presence of Christ, in all its wonder, *specifically* shape us?

Matthew helps us toward the answer to this question as he ends his Gospel with these words. "All authority in heaven and on earth has been given to me. Go therefore and make disciples of all nations, baptizing them in the name of the Father and of the Son and of the Holy Spirit, and teaching them to obey everything that I have commanded you. And remember, I am with you always, to the end of the age" (28:18–20).

Note that Matthew offers no ascension *story*, neither a mere statement as in the longer ending of Mark's Gospel nor the twice-narrated story found in Luke-Acts. Matthew makes no direct reference to the miracle, as John does. Matthew ends with Jesus and his disciples on the mountain.

But just here, on the mountain, the Ascension is presented. Consider the setting. Jesus led the disciples up to the top of a mountain. It is a small detail, but recall that Matthew has structured his story of Jesus to remind readers of Moses all the way through. From the flight to Egypt for safety, through the giving of Jesus' law on the mountain, up to the Ascension, Jesus has been recapitulating or re-covering the career of the great deliverer of God's people.

Now, on the mountain, the life of Jesus echoes the final ascent of Moses that ends the book of Deuteronomy. Moses went up—he ascended!—to the top of the mountain, where he died and was buried by God in a place where no one could find him.

At just this instant, the comparison ends. Moses leaves; Jesus does not. Moses transferred his leadership to Joshua as he himself was removed from the people of Israel not only by his death, but by deliberate divine intervention as God himself buries Moses secretly to prevent the people from worshiping at his grave.

Matthew, after drawing positive comparisons all the way through his Gospel, ends on this note of contrast. Where Moses' leadership comes to its end, Jesus' leadership persists with a new command: "Make disciples. Baptize and teach." Moses departs. Jesus remains present with a promise: "I am with you always." These words complicate the Ascension in Matthew's story.

Yet even if the Ascension is not specifically narrated, Matthew's readers are clear: they already know that Jesus' withdrawal is about to take place. As readers we should by now be able to see that the Ascension is implied in every word Jesus speaks from the mountain. Consider Jesus' last words carefully.

He begins with an announcement. "All authority has been given to me." Jesus uses the prophet Daniel's language of the exaltation of the Son of Man. The authority Jesus speaks of is conferred when the Son of Man comes with the clouds into God's presence. It is the language of heavenly reign. It is the language of the Ascension.

Drawing on his authority, he then commands: "Go. Make Disciples. Baptize. Teach." The new community, constituted by its alternative confession that the crucified and risen one has been publicly exalted to the status of Lord and God, has been given its orders. The Ascension underwrites the church's mission. The coming of the Holy Spirit—without whom the mission cannot begin—is not to be seen as a new act of God as much as the earthly echo of the heavenly enthronement of the victorious Son of Man. This is the language of mission that will form the backbone of the book of Acts, with its riveting account of the spread of the gospel throughout Jerusalem and the surrounding regions of Judea and Samaria, and eventually even in Rome itself.

And finally, the ascended Lord promises: "Remember that I am always with you." Luke and John, in their unique ways, tell us that this promise is fulfilled in the coming of the Holy Spirit, who is the Spirit of the risen one. This promise requires Jesus' literal absence in order to take effect.

Why then does Matthew omit the miracle that Luke narrates twice? An answer is beginning to emerge. Where Luke includes it to stress the reign of Jesus, perhaps Matthew, after signaling it to his readers, omits its narration lest it be seen to weaken the concluding promise of Jesus' presence.

Perhaps Matthew tells of the Ascension in this manner because he worries his readers will have the same trouble as the disciples just before Jesus addresses them. On the mountain they see Jesus, they worship Jesus, *but some doubted* (Matthew 28:17). What is there to doubt? The man was dead and is now in front of them, alive and well! The miracle draws observant Jews to worship this man. How could some doubt? What are they doubting?

Together, we have spent six chapters thinking about Jesus' absence, and its meaning. Jesus' earthly work of atonement is done, and his heavenly work of reigning has begun. We have attempted to live into its reality. Because Jesus really has withdrawn from us in his body, we confess and forgive. We have tiered loyalties and upside-down notions of victory. We celebrate. We pray for brothers and sisters we have never seen. We pray for their strength in martyrdom, even as such a possibility may one day visit us. But we doubt, too, do we not? We have seen evidence of the ascended Christ, yet we doubt.

And in this doubt we are faced with Jesus' note of promise: "Remember that I am with you always." Right here, in the midst of Matthew's affirmation of the Ascension, is Matthew's comforting words of promise to us doubters. This is the paradox of absence and presence and one in which Matthew's Jesus invites us to find comfort. When we turn to another narrative from Luke, that of Cleopas and his unnamed companion on the way to Emmaus on the first Easter Sunday, we begin to see inklings of living the paradox.

As we join the Emmaus travelers on their dry and dusty seven-mile journey, we intrude on a conversation. They were talking with each other about all that had happened over the last three days. Friday's still sharp tragedy is set alongside Sunday morning's bizarre reports. On Friday, Jesus died. On Sunday, the women said he lived again. What is going on? Has grief robbed our women of their sanity? Whatever their questions, talking wasn't going to help them make sense of what, on the face of it, was a ridiculous tale. Death *is the* final departure. Jesus could not have been restored to life. And yet, what else could they do but talk?

As we eavesdrop, we are tempted to speculate about what's really driving the conversation. Luke doesn't say. He leaves a curious textual gap. In his commentary, John Calvin suggests that Cleopas and his companion talked to shield themselves from the full offence of the Cross. They talked, in other words, to prevent their psyches from being completely overwhelmed by the awful reality that their Rabbi and Master had been betrayed, handed over, tortured, and murdered.

Calvin then presses further. Could the Emmaus disciples have talked to distract themselves from the fact that they did nothing to prevent the injustice; that they were in some way complicit? As psychologically suggestive as Calvin is at this point, and while the text might hint at this, the text does not seem to justify it.

Calvin's suggestion may well be right, but it isn't exclusive. There's no single way to describe the motives that drove the conversation between Cleopas and his companion. The explanation is both more straightforward and more complex. When we grieve together, we talk. We remember and we regret. Why would the Emmaus disciples' conversation be any different? However mixed their motives, they did not journey to Emmaus in silence. Nor did they try to distract themselves by talking about something else. They were, Luke tells us, "talking about all these things."

We are permitted to overhear their conversation— recounted for the sake of the stranger who joins them—and a mindset beyond that of simple grief is revealed. Although they had heard the women's announcement that Jesus had been raised, they had not yet come to believe. But it is clear from their conversation that they did not not-believe either. Theirs is a conversation on the knife-edge between faith and doubt. Their questions are honest ones. They are living in tension.

Whatever their psychological state, the desire that lay behind their conversation was holy. And because it was, says Calvin, God found favor in it: "We ought, at least, to hold it as certain, that when we inquire about Christ, if this be done from a modest desire . . . the door is opened for him to assist us; nay, we may also say that we then call for himself to be our Teacher."

Why do we consider this tension to be hopeful? Because two disciples, somewhere on the way between Jerusalem and Emmaus, were somewhere on the way from unbelief to faith. Because two disciples were talking and while they were laying bare their souls to each other, Jesus came and made to journey along with them. As they wrestled with his absence, Jesus became present.

Yet they do not recognize Jesus. Luke tells us that "their eyes were kept from recognizing him." How interesting! When Mark's Gospel relates this story, it implies a change in *Jesus*. Mark says that Jesus appeared to them in a different form (*en hetero morphé*).

Luke's Gospel reports no such thing. For Luke, it is not Jesus who is obscured, but the minds of the disciples that remain darkened. Their eyes, says Luke in a literal—if wooden—translation, *were held*. If you have the curious image of an angel's hands over the Emmaus disciples' eyes, you are reading Luke rightly.

For Luke, the Jesus who walked with them on the road was the Jesus who was crucified. The same heart that stopped on Friday afternoon was there and pumping once again. With them. And yet they did not see. As far as they were concerned, the Lord was still absent. He was still dead. Reports to the contrary, perhaps even their own hopes to the contrary, Cleopas and his companion knew Jesus was gone and would not be returning.

Yet, Jesus was there with them—partially perhaps to render a judgment on their unbelief. "Oh how foolish you are and slow of heart to believe," says the stranger in response to their story. A rather stern rebuke. Perhaps your first instinct, like mine, is to defend the disciples here. *Why are you so hard on them Jesus? A few words of comfort would go a long way here!* is what we wish to say. To us, the disciples are in the midst of the profoundest grief overlaid with a good measure of guilt. They need healing words. *Their unbelief is hardly their fault*, we want to add. *Faced with the overwhelming reality of a crucified body, dead and buried, isn't theirs the most appropriate response when others start raving about angels and resurrections? Can't you cut them a little slack? Let them in on the secret?*

But Jesus doesn't let them in. No slack is given; no short-cut to revelation offered. Their unbelief is culpable. To be remedied, it must first be acknowledged. The disciples have not responded in belief to the witness of the Scriptures as Jesus taught them. Cleopas and his companion should have known before the events of Thursday night and Friday unfolded, because Jesus prepared them to understand that the way to glory is the way of suffering.

But if their unbelief is culpable, Jesus' judgment is restorative rather than condemning. For when the disciples realize that they are "foolish and slow of heart to believe," they are now ready to hear again. Helpless now, they cast themselves on the mercy of this stranger. Now, having undergone the gracious judgment of the just Judge, they are ready to receive. And Jesus, still a stranger to them, opens the book.

Then Jesus, beginning with Moses and all the prophets, Luke tells us, interprets for these disciples the Scriptures in the light of himself and himself in the light of the Scriptures. The disciples are reminded again how to read the Law and the Prophets. What to look for—who to look for—there. But this is more than a first-century crash course "Bible survey." For as the stranger opens the book to their as yet held eyes, their hearts begin to burn. And he is a stranger no longer. He has become a guest.

The disciples desire to offer this stranger—this guest—their hospitality. The day is ending; Cleopas and his companion have reached their lodgings. The stranger makes to go on. Intrigued by the ease with which the stranger seems to know and interpret the Scriptures, the disciples invite him to stop with them for the evening. As the stranger becomes a guest, he accepts the offer of hospitality and he goes in with them.

But he does not remain a guest. No sooner had the door closed behind them, than this stranger who knew the Scriptures and all about Jesus, this stranger who should have been no stranger at all, assumed the role of host.

Rather than waiting to be served the evening meal, Jesus took bread, blessed and broke it, and gave it to the disciples. Early Christian commentators on this passage suggest that what takes place here is a Eucharistic meal. Perhaps. What we do know is that the three sat down to supper and the fourfold movement of taking, blessing, breaking, and giving is provided by Luke to recall the Last Supper and to remind readers of that central rite of Christian worship.

He took the bread, blessed it, broke it, and gave it to them. And their eyes were opened. And they saw that this stranger was no stranger at all. And they understood why their hearts burned as he opened the Scriptures to them. They knew him in the breaking of the bread.

And he vanished from their sight.

Here we come to the central question provoked by this strange story. Why did he vanish? Again we find Calvin's response to be especially inviting: "[B]y the sudden departure, he taught them that they must seek him elsewhere than in the world, because the completion of the new life was his ascension into heaven."

Jesus, in other words, was no longer going to be directly present to the disciples as before. He would soon be taken from them. After the Ascension, if the disciples were to see

Jesus again—if their eyes were to be opened—they would have to learn to look for Jesus elsewhere.

The presence of Jesus that comforted our doubt in Matthew now becomes the absence of Jesus that drives our belief to search for him—elsewhere, in unexpected places, and in humility as our eyes might be held.

But where on earth is elsewhere? We grew up singing an Easter song that answered that question like this: "You ask me how I know he lives? He lives within my heart!" The heart— the inner life—was the place where disciples would encounter Jesus. Are we to follow Origen in this regard or Martin Luther who came close to saying this on a few occasions? It is a defining understanding of at least some forms of Protestantism that our awareness of God is evoked by a mystical inner awareness of Jesus.

Strikingly, Luke's story doesn't speak of the heights of mystical ecstasy. He is far more mundane and material. Our challenge to live the paradox of the Ascension—the comfort of presence and the drive of absence—could easily be forsaken if we get bound up in the debates of Christendom over the four simple words, "This is my body." This is not to impugn such debates, because such debates are evidence of the paradox and, therefore, in some sense, they are formative, as well.

Yet lost in the debates can be the Johannine Jesus' simple, if graphic, invitation to eat his flesh and drink his blood. To feed on his life. John's Jesus leaves no room for metaphor. Jesus gives us no theory of the sacraments. He says, clearly and shockingly, "Those who eat my flesh and drink my blood, abide in me, and I in them" (John 6:56). Imagine being in the middle of the Prayer of Humble Access in the Episcopal

Book of Common Prayer and praying these words: "Grant us therefore, gracious Lord, so to eat the flesh of thy dear Son, Jesus Christ, and to drink his blood. . . ." Now suppose a three-year-old sitting upon his mother's lap looks up at her and says, "Wait a minute. Drink his blood?" How does one explain that to a precocious preschooler?

Or to a grown-up new convert, for that matter? You can't explain what it means to drink the blood of Jesus! Rather, the act itself is its own explanation. For in this act, whether simple or ornate, Christians—regardless of their very different understandings of what is actually happening—have met Jesus for two millennia. Here we remember, we give thanks, and we feed on Christ "by faith, in our hearts with thanksgiving."

Likewise, Christians cannot explain the ascension paradox of absence and presence to those outside the narrative, except by living the shape of this practice. Like Luke, this phrase is far more mundane and material. To put it simply, we eat together and foster in situations of absence the presence of Jesus. Christians do this without even thinking about it. We somehow know that when a funeral is held in our local churches, usually the reception is also. The funeral is over; the body is buried. The loved one's absence is even more telling. But out come the sandwiches. We talk. We comfort one another. And in that practice, unintentionally, unconsciously, but undoubtedly shaped by the Ascension, we are practicing the presence of Jesus in the face of absence.

But the family goes home and the remains of the sandwiches, pies, and coffee get cleaned up. What do Christians do? They take casseroles to the grieving family. They invite them over for dinner. They share coffee; they eat; they talk; they grieve;

they are comforted. Because Jesus is with them. Christians mourn with the elements of celebration.

Mundane examples? Most certainly. But *material* examples shaped by Eucharistic presence and thus the Ascension, too. It's essential here not to de-emphasize the sacramental nature of the Eucharist. That meal *is different.* If we consider the Eucharist as simply a common meal, then common meals remain simply common. But, if we are shaped by a robust Eucharistic practice that emphasizes its difference, then our common meals are charged with the residual grace of Eucharist. We have fed on Christ at Eucharist and thus are living in the energy of his life—even as we eat together. This is why we ought to celebrate Eucharist frequently: so that we carry Jesus from this meal, where the veil between us and the ascended Jesus is thinnest, to the places he seems most absent.

Yet this miniparadox of mourning with the elements of celebration only challenges us to live into one side of the paradox of the Ascension. How can we think of the flipside? How do we practice absence in the face of presence?

Paul tells us that Christ is at the right hand of the Father and that our lives are hidden with Christ in God (Colossians 3:1–3). In the face of the presence of suffering and evil, Christians are reminded that the absent Christ, the ascended Christ, is our safety. Christians are shaped by this side of the ascension paradox in times of local church worship when it is as though we have moved into another realm—for we have. Christians foster absence in a visible way. Could those of us with earnest doubts of faith, some may even call them seekers, find an appropriate entrance into the Christian narrative in such a worship experience? Pray to God, yes!

These two avenues of paradoxical living—mourning with celebration and fostering visible absence—are shaped by the ascended Jesus. How? Because Jesus made the hearts of those who mourned and those who doubted burn even though their eyes were held. Welcome to the challenge of the Ascension as followers of Christ: by celebrating, witnessing, confessing, forgiving, deconstructing, cruciform winning, being visibly absent, and mourning with celebration, we make hearts of those who do not yet see him *burn* for the ascended Jesus.

DISCUSSION QUESTIONS

1. Why might some of the disciples have doubted even in the face of the Resurrection?

2. How can your group or church live into the paradox of celebration and mourning?

3. How can your group or church foster the absence of Jesus in a dangerous world?

4. What Emmaus Roads are you currently walking? In other words, are there situations where you are expecting God to work when in reality the work of the ascended Jesus has already been done, but we haven't noticed?

5. The Eucharist cannot be explained. Instead it must be lived. Do you have such a sacramental view of the Eucharist?

Benediction

[May] He grant to all of you to believe on Him who
rose again, and to look for Him who is gone up, and
is to come again, (to come, but not from the earth; for
be on your guard, O man, because of the deceivers
who are to come;) Who sitteth on high, and is here
present together with us, *beholding the order of each, and
the steadfastness of his faith.* For think not that because
He is now absent in the flesh, He is therefore absent
also in the Spirit. He is here present in the midst of
us . . . ready to present those who are coming to baptism, and all of you, in the Holy Ghost to the Father,
and to say, *Behold, I and the children whom God hath given
Me*—To whom be glory for ever. Amen.

                      —Cyril of Jerusalem

Appendix

Now that the practical and formative points have been made, let us return to the basic premise. If the ascension of Jesus is as important as we have outlined in this book, let us consider again why so many contemporary Christians think so little about it.

Here is our dilemma—a dilemma that explains the silence in our own teaching and preaching. We have no trouble with the other Christological miracles—the incarnation of God in Mary's womb and the bodily resurrection of Jesus from the grave. Yet when it comes to the Ascension, we get bogged down by the funny picture of dangling feet. Do we really believe that? Don't we treat the Ascension like an absentminded great uncle—the one we can't simply exclude from the family reunion without being both rude and cruel? But he's a bit of an embarrassment, isn't he? So, let's welcome him in and shuffle him off to a corner where he won't bother anyone and hope that he stays quiet until he leaves.

Do you sometimes feel that way, too? If you do, perhaps you are ready for a way out. What if we could discount the Ascension without discrediting Christian faith? What if the Ascension is the bathwater to the gospel's baby?

Let's begin with the obvious: only Luke narrates the Ascension. Whatever theological points are being made, they're Luke's idiosyncrasies. The ascension of Jesus is briefly mentioned in the longer ending of Mark's Gospel, which was not part of the original text. The rest of the Gospels, Paul's epistles, and the later New Testament writings seem, at first, to be silent at this point.

This provides us with an attractive and easy exit. We can lump the ascension stories of Luke and Acts in with the other "hard parts" of the Bible. Because of their paucity, they can be safely ignored without compromising the central claims of the gospel. If it's not part of the New Testament as a whole, if both the story and the theology are uniquely Luke's, perhaps we can leave the Ascension alone after giving it a respectful nod on Sunday mornings.

At first glance, this two-pronged argument is quite powerful. Only Luke's writings narrate the event of the Ascension. What's more, when readers compare Luke's two versions, their differences suggest, at least at first glance—and maybe even after a more thorough reading—that Luke is using literature to make a theological point. That he's not reporting history. Questions around the reliability of Luke's story at this point cause some simply to back away from it.

This criticism gets something right. No one save Luke narrates the Ascension—at least to the detail that he does. But criticism errs by jumping to the conclusion that the event is absent from the rest of the New Testament. In fact, close reading reveals that the Ascension is presupposed or presumed throughout much of the New Testament. So if the criticism is to be taken as conclusive, then critics must go on to offer a persuasive account of those passages written by the other three evangelists, Paul, and other New Testament writers that take the Ascension for granted, or rely heavily upon it to make other theological and/or moral points. It's a mistake to infer from the observation that only Luke narrated the Ascension that only Luke knew of it or, for some theological reason, required it.

But is Luke more interested in "theology-though-literature"? Does he exaggerate a minor New Testament theme for theological reasons? Yes, Luke is not interested in the mere reporting of events (and no one before the nineteenth century would hold Luke to this peculiarly modern standard of history writing). Luke is primarily a theologian, using narrative to describe who God is and what God is like. Luke is not a dispassionate journalist engaged in reportage. He is an evangelist determined to show to his readers the reliability and significance of the gospel.

For Luke, whether Jesus ascended on Easter Day as he appears to do in Luke's Gospel, or forty days later as told by the book of Acts, is secondary to whether he was "taken up" at all. And he tells us from the beginning that he relies upon eyewitness testimony for both accounts. Luke, like any historian, whether ancient or modern, is dependent upon primary sources—witnesses to events. Luke, like any historian, whether ancient or modern, shapes his source notes toward disclosing a coherent story. In Luke's case, the resulting narrative is the Good News that God has conquered the enemies of humanity in and through Jesus of Nazareth. Whether in his Gospel or in Acts, Luke does not offer "theology-through-literature" but "theology-through-history."

The New Testament evidence, then, suggests precisely the opposite conclusion from that suggested by some critics. Far from being a dispensable invention peculiar to Luke, the Ascension is foundational to the entire New Testament and, in a variety of both implicit and explicit ways, this foundational importance drips off almost every page. The problem is not that the Ascension isn't there, but that we have been trained to ignore it.

So, disconnecting the Ascension (or Luke) from the New Testament isn't easy. Maybe the story itself is the problem. The language of Jesus being "taken up" seems to be rooted in a view of the universe that places God "up" in heaven, human beings and the material world "beneath" him in the middle, and the realm of ghosts and witless spirits lower yet in Hades or hell.

Today we know that the universe is not to be understood in so "vertical" a way. It is clear to us as moderns that wherever God is, wherever Jesus went, Jesus isn't dangling his feet just out of sight, over our heads. "Heaven" is not up there, and we have advanced in our understanding of how the world works beyond the point where Luke's story is plausible.

The naturalist challenge raises the stakes even further. As a worldview, Naturalism presupposes that every effect can be (and eventually will be) explained without recourse to the supernatural. "God," in other words, is never a legitimate explanation for any natural event. To put it bluntly, this criticism avers that God, if God exists, does not intervene in the natural world.

The natural world functions on basic laws of cause and effect. There are gaps in our knowledge. We don't know all about quarks, quasars, quantum mechanics, and lots of other mysterious items and events. But physicists don't start spouting "God" whenever they run into these gaps. And rightly so. For to do so would stop the investigation. They theorize, experiment, test, and publish in the hopes that they will fill these gaps.

What does Naturalism have to do with the ascension of Jesus? The Ascension, it explains, like all miracle stories, is either a legend or a prescientific (and ultimately false) explanation for natural occurrence. We cannot know what happened. For the only account we have is plainly impossible on the face of it. We know too much about how the world works—far more than the authors of the New Testament—to take its miracle stories at face value. Literally speaking, the Ascension could not have happened.

According to the Naturalist, whether we're talking about a vertical universe or a miraculous one, the ascension of Jesus did not occur the way Luke describes it. The description itself depends on a false view of the universe.

Yet, Bishop N.T. Wright offers a stunning counter here. When inhabitants of the first century spoke of a two- or three-decker universe, they did so in just the same way that we speak of the sun "rising" in the East. "To speak of someone 'going up to heaven,'" Wright offers, "by no means implied that the person concerned had (a) become a primitive space-traveler and (b) arrived, by that means, at a different location within the space-time universe." Yes, the Ascension requires Christian reflection on cosmology. But to believe in the Ascension as an event in the life of Jesus does not require that we presuppose a worldview in which heaven is "up," the grave is "down," and we are somewhere in the "middle."

Now, trickier is the argument that the Ascension is a miracle story and we know that miracles don't happen. This challenge suggests that the ascension accounts must meet a skeptic's burden of proof before we may believe it happened. What else can be said but that according to the evidence we have, Luke narrated the Ascension based on the eyewitnesses he consulted, and other New Testament writers assume that it occurred. In both cases, they believed the Ascension was an event in the life of Jesus. Some of those eyewitnesses wagered their lives on the fact that Jesus actually ascended.

For the skeptic, that may not be enough. If that's the case, then we cannot meet his burden of proof. Christian apologists have shown it is not necessarily irrational to believe in miracles, but that doesn't in itself prove this miracle. By the same token, though, even claims to what we ate for breakfast are dubitable! That's the problem with history. Each event is fundamentally unique. As a result, there will never be any set of evidence that is beyond all doubt. All we have are the source materials and the witnesses.

The above challenges are all relatively modern, depending heavily on two-century-old historical critical reading of the New Testament or directly descending from David Hume's argument discounting miracles. Even Christians who struggle with the Ascension, further, will find miracles hard to embrace.

But what if a challenge to the Ascension as an event can be mounted from within the faith? We can detect one version in the writings of Origen of Alexandria, a third-century Christian theologian, and it continues to pop up from time to time, especially in Christian mystical writings. If this last challenge is true, then the skeptical power of the other three is actually overcome.

This challenge says that the Ascension had nothing to do with Jesus' body. It was, rather, how Jesus left his body behind.

It treats the Ascension as an example—a particularly good, or even the best, one to be sure—for the ascent of the soul to God. Just as Jesus left material creation, his body, and perhaps even his humanity behind in order to commune with immaterial Spirit, so should we. The Ascension ceases to be about the restoration of humanity and creation to fellowship with God and becomes instead about the rescue of humanity from creation to God.

This rereading seems to owe more to Plato and Plotinus than to the Jewish milieu in which the New Testament was written. But it's still attractive. If the Ascension really is about Jesus' soul and not about his body, then the picture of dangling feet just goes away, as do critical questions about the New Testament, cosmology, and miracles. And life is made a whole lot easier, because Luke's story is reduced to metaphor. Origen's particular understanding may well be as implausible today as Luke's story. But his intention has abided across time. Whenever we "demythologize" the Ascension—chip away at the supposedly legendary, mythological, just plain wrong outer shell to get to the spiritual, ultimate, true core—we are following Origen, even when we use the modern methods of biblical criticism. The problem is, we have solved the Ascension's problems and diluted its offensiveness by emptying it of its plain meaning. And one cannot simply imagine early Christians wagering their lives on such a weakened account.

Critics may say that biblical, cosmological, naturalistic, and metaphorical challenges have been caricatured. No doubt, that is true. But this is not an academic apology for the rationality and plausibility of the Ascension accounts. The book's aim—to reflect on the Ascension and its implications for contemporary followers of Jesus—is far more modest. It offers equally incomplete responses to inadequate descriptions. Critics aren't silenced, but hopefully a space is opened in which this book's two organizing questions might be asked.

Notes

3   *The Ascension is the festival which confirms*   Quoted by J.G. Davies, *He Ascended into Heaven* (London: Lutherworth 1958), 170.

5   *And it invites hard questions from the start.*   Some of those hard questions are important, but ancillary to the St. Luke's story. They deal with the story's plausibility and our credulity. While the main ones are traced here, more avenues are offered in the appendix.

13   *"[This] is how the clues God leaves sometimes work*   Lauren F. Winner, *Girl Meets God* (New York: Random House, 2008), 57.

19   *The Gospel writers agree*—Though they agree on the agency of the Spirit, the manner of the agency is differently described. Where Matthew and Luke speak of Jesus being led, as though the Spirit is in the wilderness beckoning to Jesus, Mark is much more graphic. For him, the Spirit actually "drives" Jesus into his first fight with the evil one.

27   *For the gift, being truly great,*   Saint John Chrysostom, *On the Epistle to the Hebrews* 2.2, as quoted in Erik M. Heen and Philip D. Kery, *Hebrews*, Ancient Christian Commentary on Scripture, vol. 10 (Downers Grove, IL: InterVarsity Press, 2005), 17.

31 *The cross conveyed degradation and death.*   See Joel B. Green,
    "Death of Jesus," in *Dictionary of Jesus and the Gospels*, ed.
    Joel B. Green, Scot McKnight and I. Howard Marshall,
    (Downers Grove, IL: IVP, 1992), 146–63, especially
    147–48.

33 *And the Surge speaks against the Cross.*   The best introduction
    to the political issues underlying this paragraph remains
    Paul Ramsey's *The Just War: Force and Political Responsibility*
    (New York: Scribners, 1968), and for the spectrum of po-
    tential ethical responses, the standard guide continues
    to be H. Richard Niebuhr's *Christ and Culture* (New York:
    Harper and Row, 1956).

34 *"[W]hat are human beings that you are mindful*   Older translations
    follow the Hebrew language, keeping the description
    individual—what is "man"? This better accentuates that
    the dignity God gives rests not on the race as much as on
    each person, regardless of whatever socially constructed
    distinctions we might like to erect.

36 *Two accounts illustrate this intentional,*   Rodney Stark, *The Rise
    of Christianity: A Sociologist Reconsiders History* (Princeton:
    Princeton University Press, 1996), 73–94.

36 *"In the face of terrible conditions,*   Andy Crouch, *Culture Making:
    Recovering Our Creative Calling* (Downers Grove, IL: Inter-
    Varsity Press, 2008), 156–57.

36 *"Many died in their stead.* Ibid., 157.

37 *Tensions that have claimed* Meg Handley, *The Violence in Nigeria: What's Behind the Conflict?* in Time. http://www. time.com/time/world/article/0,8599,1971010,00.html (accessed April 13, 2010).

39 *He was carried up unto heaven,* Cyril of Alexandria, *Commentary on the Gospel of Saint Luke,* trans. R. Payne Smith (Astoria, NY: Studion, 1983), 620.

43 *"the finale of his earthly sojourn* Joel B. Green, *The Gospel of Luke,* NICNT (Grand Rapids: Eerdmans, 1997), 861.

44 *Moses* went up Again the language of ascent.

46 *The coming of the Holy Spirit,* Jesus is more, of course. Having received this empowering Spirit, the task of telling the Good News of Jesus will follow almost automatically. The disciples will tell what they had seen and heard; they won't be able to stop themselves.

47 *No wonder that within two or three decades,* An early hymn is quoted by Paul in his letter to the church in Philippi. See Philippians 2:5–11.

52 *"The Jesus who suffered and died* Green, *The Gospel of Luke,* 862.

57 *He showed them that after his resurrection* Gregory the Great, *Forty Gospel Homilies,* 26, as quoted in *Cistercian Studies* (Kalamazoo: Cistercian Publications, 1973), 123:201.

61 *The Johannine location and nature* Some readers might believe there is a simple assumption that Thomas' confession is an *ascension* confession. Coming one week after the resurrection of Jesus and before the Ascension, someone could argue that it's not. But consider the following reasons for an ascension reading: First, John has no ascension story; rather, for him, the Resurrection *is* the Ascension (or at least, it's beginning). Remember his words to Mary at the tomb? "Stop clinging to Me, for I have not yet *ascended* to the Father. . . . Go to My brethren and say to them 'I ascend to My Father and to your Father'" John 20:17. Further, the content of the confession—"My Lord and my God"—is an affirmation of the reign of Jesus that in the New Testament *presumes* the Ascension. Thomas' confession *only* makes full sense as an ascension confession.

62 *Any attempt to nuance* Specifically, Leviticus 19:28, which reads, "You shall not make any gashes in your flesh for the dead or tattoo any marks upon you: I am the Lord."

67 *"we keep the eighth day* *The Epistle of Barnabas*, trans. J.B. Lightfoot, http://www.carm.org/epistle-of-barnabus (accessed March 11, 2010).

67 *Mary had even laid hold of him* This is the clear implication of Jesus' words in John 20:17.

70 *Make no mistake:* John Updike, "Seven Stanzas at Easter," in *Telephone Poles and Other Poems* (New York: Alfred A Knopf, 1963), 72–73.

71   *"The only begotten Word of God* Cyril of Alexandria, *Letter
     to Acacius* 18 (ACO 1.1.4, p. 46), as quoted by Peter
     Widdicombe, "The Wounds and the Ascended Body: The
     Marks of Crucifixion in the Glorified Christ from Justin
     Martyr to John Calvin," *Laval Théologique et Philosophique*
     59,1 (2003),143.

71   *"The divine one, equal to the Father,* All quotes and allusions
     in this paragraph and the next are taken from Peter
     Widdicombe, ibid, 143.

73   *Mel Gibson's* The Passion of the Christ Mel Gibson, dir.
     The Passion of the Christ (Los Angeles: Icon Productions,
     2004).

77   *But as in the persecutions*   Cyril of Alexandria, "On the
     Clause, And Shall Come in Glory to Judge the Quick
     and the Dead; Of Whose Kingdom There Shall Be No
     End," trans. Edwin Hamilton Gifford, *Nicene and Post-
     Nicene Fathers*, Second Series, Vol. 7, ed. Philip Schaff
     and Henry Wace, eds. http://www.ccel.org/ccel/schaff/
     npnf207.ii.xix.html (accessed April 13, 2010).

79   *They would be tolerated too,* And of course, when the Jews
     did revolt they were crushed and dispersed.

85   *Eighty and six years* Polycarp, *The Martyrdom of Polycarp*,
     trans. J.B. Lightfoot, http://www.carm.org/apologetics/
     lost-books/letter-smyrnaeans-or-martyrdom-polycarp.
     (accessed February 16, 2010).

86 *"[F]or Stephen to commit his spirit* Jaroslav Pelikan, *Acts,* Brazos
    Theological Commentary on the Bible (Grand Rapids:
    Brazos, 2006), 107.

88 *"fight through their prayer to God*   Origen, *Origen Against
    Celsus, VIII.73. Ante-Nicene Fathers,* vol. 4. A. Cleveland
    Coxe, ed. (Grand Rapids: Eerdmans, n.d.) http://www.
    ccel.org/ccel/schaff/anf04.vi.ix.viii.lxxiii.html (accessed
    April 13, 2010).

89 *Some forgiveness is only safe*   See Miroslav Volf, *Exclusion and
    Embrace: A Theological Exploration of Identity, Otherness, and
    Reconciliation* (Nashville, TN: Abingdon Press, 1996),
    especially ch. 7.

90 *"Latimer! Latimer! Latimer!*   Latimer's words are taken from
    Christopher Bryan, *Render Unto Caesar: Jesus, the Early Church
    and the Roman Superpower* (Oxford: Oxford University
    Press, 2005), 126.

91 *"I die the King's good servant*   More is often remembered,
    perhaps because of the popularity of *A Man for All Seasons,*
    as saying "but God's first." As far as we can find, however,
    the conjunction he actually spoke was "and."

93 *Jesus stirred up their minds* Cyril of Alexandria, *Commentary
    on the Gospel of Saint Luke,* 617.

99 *In his commentary, John Calvin suggests* John Calvin, *Commentary
    on Matthew, Mark, Luke,* vol. 3 , trans. Rev. William Pringle,

http://www.ccel.org/ccel/calvin/calcom33.ii.xlviii.html
(accessed February 16, 2010).

100 *"We ought, at least, to hold it* Ibid., http://www.ccel.org/
ccel/calvin/calcom33.ii.xlviii.html (accessed March 11,
2010).

103 *"[B]y the sudden departure,* Ibid., http://www.ccel.org/ccel/cal-
vin/calcom33.ii.xlix.html. (accessed February 16, 2010).

109 *[May] He grant to all of you* Cyril of Jerusalem, *Catechetical
Lectures,* 14.30, NPNF2, vol. 7, http://www.ccel.org/ccel/
schaff/npnf207.ii.xviii.html. (accessed March 3, 2010).

111 *Yet when it comes* It is a fairly common medieval artistic
trope to present the Ascension as the disciples and Mary
gazing up at a pair of feet emerging from the bottom of a
cloud.

112 *In fact, close reading reveals* Consider the following passages: Matthew 26:64 (and its reiteration in Mark, 14:62);
Luke 9:31, 51; John 3:13, 6:62, 14:2, 20:17; Acts 2:34,
3:21, 5:31, 7:56; Romans 8:34, 10:6; Ephesians 1:20; 4:8–
10; Philippians 2:9, 3:14; Colossians 3:1; 1 Timothy 3:16;
Hebrews 1:3, 4:14, 6:19–20, 7:26, 8:1–2, 9:11, 9:24; 1
Peter 3:21–22; and Revelation 11:12, 12:5.

113 *And he tells us from the beginning* People interested in New
Testament criticism may well find in Richard Bauckham's
large yet engaging book *Jesus and the Eyewitnesses: The Gospels
as Eyewitness Testimony* (Grand Rapids: Eerdmans, 2006) a

powerful argument for the reliability of such testimony as historical evidence.

115 *"To speak of someone 'going up to heaven,'"* N.T. Wright, *The Resurrection of the Son of God* (Philadelphia: Augsberg Fortress), 655. This is another massive work, and like Bauckham's, it is also well worth the effort!

Acknowledgments

TIM'S ACKNOWLEDGMENTS

One of the ironies of a writer's life is that when one feels most indebted to a number of people for the successful completion of a project, expressions of thanks ring hollow all the more. The only thing worse than inadequate words in this instance, though, is silence. So here goes. The gestation and birth of this project followed a typical route. An idea became a sermon series, then a book proposal, and now a book. For helping me to see that process through, I wish to thank Chris Holmes, Chris Banman, the vestry and congregation of St. Margaret's Anglican Church, and the staff and campers of Star Lake Lodge. Two "bookends" deserve special thanks: Scot McKnight who almost two years ago now, recommended that I consider Paraclete Press as a home for this book, and Lil Copan, my kind and careful editor, who stuck with the project until I was able to complete it.

As writing the book entered its final stages, real life interrupted in a sad and surprising way. Many rallied to support Rachel and me during our crisis. I hope those left anonymous will see themselves included alongside our parents, Cornie Wiens and Ellard and Kathryn Perry, and these friends: Revel and Helen Robinson, Dorothy Young, Elaine and José Pinto, and the Rev. Jennifer Sisson. You were a particular "means of grace" at pivotal places, and I am grateful.

Last, the Rev. David and Ruth Widdicombe, and the Rev. Greg and Rachel Bloomquist provided pastoral care that was life-giving and sustaining. To these dear friends I dedicate this book.

AARON'S ACKNOWLEDGMENTS

The opportunity to contribute to this book came as a surprise, and my acknowledgments reflect this surprise. What ability I have to offer contributions was shaped in a local church where preaching was valued and practice was emphasized. As such, I am thankful to my wife, Heather, who, since the beginning of our relationship, has heard every sermon I've preached at least three times. I am also grateful to my parents, Ellard and Kathryn, and friends Gary and Diane Sawyer and Skeet and Arline Wales who heard scattered forms of sermons, even ones on the Ascension, before Sunday's final form. Their thoughtful questions and encouragement have helped to shape my love for preaching.

About Paraclete Press

WHO WE ARE

Paraclete Press is a publisher of books, recordings, and DVDs on Christian spirituality. Our publishing represents a full expression of Christian belief and practice—from Catholic to Evangelical, from Protestant to Orthodox.

We are the publishing arm of the Community of Jesus, an ecumenical monastic community in the Benedictine tradition. As such, we are uniquely positioned in the marketplace without connection to a large corporation and with informal relationships to many branches and denominations of faith.

WHAT WE ARE DOING
Books

Paraclete publishes books that show the richness and depth of what it means to be Christian. Although Benedictine spirituality is at the heart of all that we do, we publish books that reflect the Christian experience across many cultures, time periods, and houses of worship. We publish books that nourish the vibrant life of the church and its people—books about spiritual practice, formation, history, ideas, and customs.

We have several different series, including the best-selling Living Library, Paraclete Essentials, and Paraclete Giants series of classic texts in contemporary English; A Voice from the Monastery—men and women monastics writing about living a spiritual life today; award-winning literary faith fiction and poetry; and the Active Prayer Series that brings creativity and liveliness to any life of prayer.

Recordings

From Gregorian chant to contemporary American choral works, our music recordings celebrate sacred choral music through the centuries. Paraclete distributes the recordings of the internationally acclaimed choir Gloriæ Dei Cantores, praised for their "rapt and fathomless spiritual intensity" by *American Record Guide*, and the Gloriæ Dei Cantores Schola, which specializes in the study and performance of Gregorian chant. Paraclete is also the exclusive North American distributor of the recordings of the Monastic Choir of St. Peter's Abbey in Solesmes, France, long considered to be a leading authority on Gregorian chant.

DVDs

Our DVDs offer spiritual help, healing, and biblical guidance for life issues: grief and loss, marriage, forgiveness, anger management, facing death, and spiritual formation.

Learn more about us at our Web site:
www.paracletepress.com, or call us toll-free at 1-800-451-5006.

YOU MAY ALSO BE INTERESTED IN . . .

THE GIVER OF LIFE
THE HOLY SPIRIT IN ORTHODOX TRADITION

Fr. John W. Oliver

Reflecting on the relationship of the Holy Spirit to the Church, the world, and the human person, Oliver looks to the biblical and liturgical tradition of Orthodox Christianity in this practical introduction designed to enrich the understanding of all Christians.

ISBN: 978-1-55725-675-1 TRADE PAPER
$15.99

THE SPIRIT UNFETTERED
PROTESTANT VIEWS ON THE HOLY SPIRIT

Edmund J. Rybarczyk, Ph.D.

After comparing Protestant views with Roman Catholic and Eastern Orthodox models, Rybarczyk explores the understandings of important figures in Protestant tradition; Luther, The Anabaptists, John Wesley, OSchleiermacher, Kuyper, Barth, as well as living theologians such as Moltmann, Pannenberg, Pinnock, and Welker.

ISBN: 978-1-55725-654-6 TRADE PAPER
$15.99

Available from most booksellers or through Paraclete Press:

www.paracletepress.com • 1-800-451-5006.

Try your local bookstore first.